TRUMPBOOK

How Digital Liberals Silenced A Nation Into Making America Hate Again

Naresh Vissa

FOREWORD BY:
Wayne Allyn Root
2008 Libertarian Vice Presidential Nominee

AFTERWORD BY:
Gerald Celente
Founder, Trends Research Institute

Naresh Vissa
TRUMPBOOK
**How Digital Liberals Silenced A Nation
Into Making America Hate Again**

ISBN-13: 978-1979115025 (Krish Publishing)
ISBN-10: 1979115028
ASIN: B075VZRX6X

WARNING!

The following content is controversial and may be considered offensive or disturbing to digital liberals.

Reader discretion is advised.

Table of Contents

TRUMPBOOK

ABOUT THE AUTHOR

Naresh Vissa is the #1 bestselling author of <u>FIFTY SHADES OF MARKETING: Whip Your Business Into Shape & Dominate Your Competition</u>, <u>PODCASTNOMICS: The Book Of Podcasting... To Make You Millions</u>, and <u>THE NEW PR: 21st Century Public Relations Strategies & Resources... To Reach Millions</u>. He is also the Founder & CEO of Krish Media & Marketing – a full service online and digital media and marketing consultancy and agency. He has worked with leading publishers, media firms and institutions such as CNN Radio, J.P. Morgan Chase, EverBank, The Institute for Energy Research, Houston Rockets, Houston Astros, the American Junior Golf Association, Agora Financial, Agora Publishing, Stansberry Research and TradeStops.

Born and raised in Houston, Texas, Vissa graduated *Magna Cum Laude* from Syracuse University's Honors Program with degrees in broadcast journalism, finance and accounting. He earned a Master's Degree from Duke University's Fuqua School of Business and is also a graduate of Hillsborough County's Backstage Pass and Mayor's Neighborhood University under the City of Tampa Mayor Bob Buckhorn.

USA Today, Yahoo!, Bloomberg, MSNBC, *Huffington*

Post, Businessweek, *MSN Money*, *Business Insider*, *India Today*, *Hindustan Times* and other domestic and international media outlets have featured Vissa.

Subscribe to Naresh Vissa's free mailing list at www.nareshvissa.com.

You can contact Naresh Vissa at Naresh at KrishMediaMarketing dot com.

Naresh Vissa

TRUMPBOOK

How Digital Liberals Silenced A Nation Into Making America Hate Again

Naresh Vissa

FOREWORD

By Wayne Allyn Root

*Host of the national television and syndicated radio shows,
"WAR Now: The Wayne Allyn Root Show" on Newsmax TV
and USA Radio Network
Bestselling Author of THE POWER OF RELENTLESS
and ANGRY WHITE MALE
Former Libertarian Vice Presidential Nominee
www.RootForAmerica.com*

Reddit Message:
*"You're a fucking moron. I hope your father gets AIDS and then
fucks you in your stupid mouth with his AIDS dick."*

My 2016 bestselling book ANGRY WHITE MALE:
How the Donald Trump Phenomenon is Changing
America—and What We Can All Do to Save the Middle
Class explained, analyzed and predicted the entire
Donald Trump election victory when no one else saw it
coming. As a card-carrying S.O.B. (son of a butcher), I
have a unique understanding of butchers, bakers and
candlestick makers. I grew up in a blue-collar New York
neighborhood of cops, firemen, nurses, mechanics, and
small business owners.

I love the middle class and small business owners (who are our country's upper middle class). I understand them. I understand how important they are to the U.S. economy.

Pew Research reports the American middle class is composed of four groups, and all of them are predominantly white. My book explains in detail why the middle class overwhelmingly supports Trump. It was titled "Angry White Male" simply because the American middle class is primarily white... and as a kid who grew up white, male and middle class, I have a unique understanding of the hopes, dreams and fears of that specific group.

The anger of almost every white middle class Trump voter has nothing to do with racism...and everything to do with economics. It's about financial survival — not race. The middle class is being targeted for extinction. It is being persecuted and wiped off the face of the earth by liberal, progressive or socialist economic policies.

The middle class and small business owners are not concerned with the color of anyone's skin. They are concerned with big taxes, big regulations, big government, illegal immigration and their use of

Obamacare, climate change, and government agencies like the EPA and the IRS to kill our jobs and redistribute our hard-earned income. Those are the reasons middle class voters are angry. Those are the reasons 63 million Americans chose Donald Trump. *Not race.*

The middle class is fighting for survival. Liberal big government policies are destroying our jobs, incomes, assets, opportunities and mobility. They are killing the American Dream. We see that our kids are being left behind. And we know giving government more power and money will make it worse.

We are screaming for help. We voted for Donald Trump out of self-defense.

The mainstream called us racist. They said we were deplorable. They shamed us all the way to the voting booths.

Yet the liberal news media never blamed my college classmate at Columbia University Barack Obama, President Bill Clinton or his wife Hillary Clinton for *anything.* They were never blamed by the mainstream media for violence started from digital liberal groups — the kind Naresh Vissa describes in this book — like antifa or Black Lives Matter. They were never blamed for disgusting signs displayed or disgraceful things said at leftist events. People chanted "death to pigs" (police) and "death to Israel." Liberal activists from coast to coast chanted hate toward every other group imaginable. Hollywood stars wished *publicly* for the assassination of President Trump. They received zero blame by the mainstream media frauds. ZERO.

Many of my friends are cops. They saw it all. They couldn't believe that digital liberals wanted to murder cops, Jews, and... President Trump. They say those things openly. They have signs saying it... yet no liberal leaders ever condemned them for their foul-mouthed behavior, threats of violence, or racism.

Don't you think President Trump has seen and heard all these death threats? Why should radical extremists on the liberal left get a pass? Why shouldn't President Trump (the man they threaten to murder) be allowed to point out that there are bad people (and violent people) on both sides?

On Twitter and Facebook, liberals by the thousands (per minute) threaten the assassination of Trump. Through Naresh's book <u>TRUMPBOOK</u>, I want everyone to see the UGLY, filthy, hateful and foul-mouthed face of digital liberals. Naresh does a great job of compiling digital liberal paranoia and responding back with logical rationale.

After I appeared on Reddit for an interview with young liberals, I received the following message:

"You're a fucking moron. I hope your father gets AIDS and then fucks you in your stupid mouth with his AIDS dick."

Lovely. Aren't digital liberals wonderful people? No hate there. No hate crimes with liberals, huh?

Many of these digital liberals are crazy America-hating commies with a disdain for free speech. They hate cops. They can't do math. As a result, they want everything "free." Of course, "free" means paid for by you and me. We pay double. We pay for ours, plus pay for their "free" healthcare through much higher taxes and premiums.

Speaking of President Obama... he and I were Columbia University Class of '83. I know all too well how mindlessly liberal the students and faculty of that institution can be, and Barack Obama is certainly no exception.

My time at Columbia made it crystal clear: liberals always believe they are morally superior. While they publicly state that their mission is to save the world from prejudice, patriotism, racism, greed, and inequality, they are, in fact, hostile and resentful towards anyone who has achieved self-made success through American values.

It is in this cesspool of intolerance that Obama and his Marxist cronies hatched a secret plan to destroy our country...

They openly hated America – calling it racist. They hated capitalism – and vowed to bring "the system down."

Obama was pre-law in the political science major – just like me. I thought I knew everyone studying political science during my four years at Columbia. Not Obama. I never met him, never saw him, never even heard of him. Strange. Same major, same career path, and graduated on the same day.

Where was he? Was he busy attending communist or socialist club meetings?

No need to guess. In his autobiography, he proudly admits attending Socialist Party meetings at Cooper Union in downtown Manhattan. He also admits to not wanting to meet anyone at Columbia who wasn't black, Hispanic, gay, or a Marxist professor. His words. So, it's possible he was so busy attending socialist / communist meetings and trying to avoid guys like me (white, straight, loved America) that our paths never crossed. Unlikely, but possible.

I have four beautiful, brilliant, perfect children. It's time to stop being nice and sugar-coating. Many digital liberals are evil and mentally ill. Many of them have publicly supported abortion until the last hours before birth, and they want to murder babies with our tax money. That literally defines radical and extreme – ironically, the words digital liberals often use to describe anyone who doesn't think like them.

These pathetic, moronic snowflakes are handing the 2018 Midterms and 2020 Election to the GOP and Trump.

It's time for patriots and the great American middle class to fight back strongly, passionately, aggressively, no holds barred. Let the battle begin!

WAR

Wayne Allyn Root

Host of the national television and syndicated radio shows, "WAR Now: The Wayne Allyn Root Show" on Newsmax TV and USA Radio Network

Bestselling Author of THE POWER OF RELENTLESS and ANGRY WHITE MALE

Former Libertarian Vice Presidential Nominee

www.RootForAmerica.com

DEDICATION

Facebook Post:

"OMG – you can't say anything important in America without a tidal wave of liberal intolerance."

I'd like to dedicate this book to:
1) Digital liberals
2) President Barack Obama
3) The year 2016
4) Non-liberal victims of cyberbullying on Facebook and other social media

1) This book goes out to the **digital liberals**, for without you, it would've been much harder to write so quickly or even impossible to concoct topics or themes. Your display of digital emotion, irrationality, intolerance, sensitivity, name-calling, and overall hatred and marginalization of people different from you made this project so quick and simple to ideate and execute.

The problem with close-minded digital liberals is that their digital mouths are always open. I'm a writer and researcher, so, in this book, I won't get into much of the name-calling ("racist", "gtfo", "stupid", "shut up," etc.) too many digital liberals utilize.

Digital liberals have loud voices, and the mainstream media is biased, so it seems like everyone agrees with them, even if they don't at all.

I look forward to your continued digital liberalization of negative reviews and comments about this book and me on Amazon. Feel free to write away in the form of reviews.

2) I think **President Barack Obama** was the best President in my lifetime (I wasn't born when Reagan was around)... better than Bill Clinton and the Bushes.

Obama gets a lot of sh*t, and I'm not sure why. The guy tried his best and has some solid results to prove it. He stunk in some areas, but who doesn't?

Under Obama's Presidency, the economy grew from -5.4% to 3.5% GDP growth. Unemployment plummeted from 8% to 5%. The deficit as a percentage of GDP tumbled from 10% to 3%.

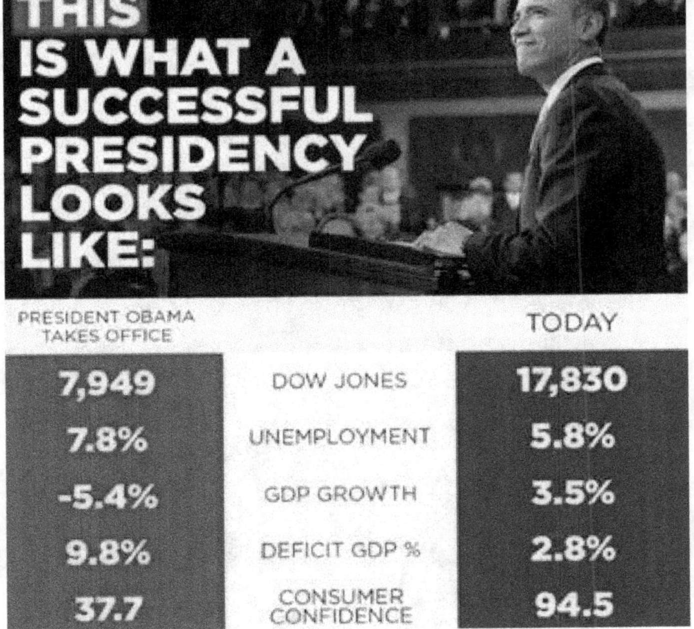

PRESIDENT OBAMA TAKES OFFICE		TODAY
7,949	DOW JONES	17,830
7.8%	UNEMPLOYMENT	5.8%
-5.4%	GDP GROWTH	3.5%
9.8%	DEFICIT GDP %	2.8%
37.7	CONSUMER CONFIDENCE	94.5

Does that mean Obama was the best ever? No.

Does that mean I agreed with his ideologies or policies on all issues? No.

In fact, President Donald Trump's victory was a reflection of Obama's failed presidency, just like George W. Bush's victory in 2000 was a reflection of Bill Clinton's failed presidency. If Americans were so happy with Obama and Bill Clinton, then they would've come out in droves to continue the course with Bill Clinton's Vice President Al Gore in 2000 or Obama's Secretary of State and Bill Clinton's wife Hillary Clinton in 2008 and 2016.

Obama and Sarah Palin paved the way for Trump and Hillary Clinton to make it so far in 2016... and Trump will pave the way for people like Mark Cuban, Kanye West, and The Rock to be taken seriously in the future.

Status quo politics is no more.

I looked up to Obama for "hope" when he was a no-name, young and intelligent politician at the Hurricane Katrina Relief efforts in 2005, and I now look up to him as a model husband and father. While he was politically weak and clueless on various issues, Senator and President Obama has always been a class act, and in President Donald Trump's own words, "a great man."

3) **2016** was one crazily insane year. The greatest team in NBA history, the Golden State Warriors, who won an NBA record 73 games – not likely to ever be broken – blew a 3-1 series lead in the NBA Finals and lost...

The European Union (EU) was set up to remain forever. British voters fooled everyone and forced Britain to leave it...

The Chicago Cubs were down 3-1 in the World Series. They came back to win it all for the first time in nearly 110 years – one week before the President Election...

2016 was a shocking year to say the least, and it was only fitting that Donald Trump came out of nowhere to be elected President of the United States.

4) As the author of this book, I also want to acknowledge **everyone who has felt bullied by reading political posts on Facebook** and other social media, which have been mostly left-wing or anti-Trump. Many of you think your friends hate you just because you voted for President Trump or because your friends know your political affiliation, even if you haven't said a damn thing.

The Left is responsible for Trump winning because the Left decided that other opinions and ways of looking at the world are unacceptable. If you call a Leftist out on his or her baseless opinion or don't agree with them, then you're labeled a freak, evil, stupid idiot, racist, xenophobe, or deplorable.

How do you think people are going to vote if you talk to them like that?

The more digital liberals whine and cry, the more the "Silent 49%" who support Trump will grow. The Silent 49% were so shamed that they let their votes do the talking.

The Election of 2016 was a wakeup call to intolerant digital liberals. They got exactly what they deserved because they were delusional enough to not even see his victory coming. It's made nearly half the country laugh, smile and proud to see digital liberal tears about the very issues they created.

Those who profess to support tolerance and equality have become the most intolerant and chauvinistic.

It's tough going against hate-filled digital liberals. They have few facts. They have few arguments. But they have a very deep emotional psychology and vocabulary of insults.

I'm not saying non-digital liberals aren't haters. Many of them are, and I share examples of them in this book too.

Republicans want to control who you screw. Democrats want you to get screwed.

So it's a battle of hate.

Hopefully, this book will resonate with your situation and give you the vote of support and confidence that you're not alone.

INTRODUCTION

Facebook Post:

"People that challenge or argue with my posts: BLOCKED!
Trump is going to Make America great again: BLOCKED!
'Respect authority': Put some respeck on this BLOCK!
'Trump is not racist': DEKCOLB (Read that backwards)!
'But he broke the law!': BLOCKING YOU FASTER
THAN THE TIME HAKEEM OLAJUWON
BLOCKED JOHN STARKS IN GAME 6 AT THE
1994 NBA FINALS!
When you say #DrainTheSwamp: KARATE CHOP
BLOCK!
'#AllLivesMatter': All BLOCKS matter!
'I don't see color': Well, you gon' see this BLOCK, boo boo!"

Ever since Donald Trump announced his candidacy for President of the United States in 2015, the U.S. political landscape has been more charged and polarizing than ever before – thanks to the ubiquity and popularity of social media. Presidents Barack Obama and Donald Trump have proven that social media has eclipsed mainstream media as a communication vehicle of choice.

There have been far more charged and vitriolic elections in the United States and worldwide. People just didn't experience them because there were no 24/7 media or social media. The periods of President Bill Clinton's sex scandal and President George W. Bush's idiotic gaffes and disastrous war in Iraq led to public outcries, but the nation didn't follow politics on such a grand scale back then because it wasn't being discussed so openly among citizens.

By nearly all statistical measures – discussed in greater detail within this book – the Election of 2016 was the most followed election in our lifetimes. That's a good trait.

Throughout the 2016 Presidential campaign – and after Trump's victory in November 2016 – I saw misinformed post after post and dumb comment after comment on social media... particularly on Facebook. People were clueless about "the system," laws, issues and players. They were making up facts, digitally yelling and screaming, bumping their chests, and crying for illegitimate reasons.

Social networks like Facebook are algorithmically controlled echo chambers that profit from confirmation bias. This is where people "socialize" with other people who think mostly like one another while getting "news" that is specifically geared toward similar tastes. Users get force-fed what they already want to hear.

We now live in a society where fake news outperforms real news because of social media. A *BuzzFeed News* analysis found that top fake election news stories generated more total engagement on Facebook than top election stories from 19 major news outlets combined.

Instead of connecting people, digital media has distorted the reality of the world. The Information Age has created technologies designed to connect and inform us, but the effect has been the opposite of intention.

Obama got new people to hit the voting booths in 2008 and 2012. Trump did the same in 2016. It's why the Election of 2016 had the most voters ever. That is not something people should be fearful of just because they did not vote for Trump.

I wrote this book to educate people on the facts: to prove that Trump's haters were actually his biggest supporters in helping him get elected... and to share some of the most thought-provoking and entertaining digital media posts I came across. A good chunk of this book consists of Facebook posts or comments that I've pasted – word-for-word – along with rebuttals and analysis. I've hidden the names and identities of all posters. They should be thankful to me for this... because there is an utter lack of critical thinking on Facebook, and it's mind-boggling.

I also wrote this book because of the criticisms and heat – and let's not forget about the praise and support too – I was getting when throwing facts and logic into online and social debate. My words incited, and I received a ton of hate, blocks and unfriends. The number of friends and friends of friends who've ganged up on me or called me every name imaginable was out of this world.

That's when I knew I was on to something...

My posts and responses were the first sample chapters that turned into this book.

One of the things I enjoy most about Facebook is having a Timeline tell me what I should be outraged and offended about...

You can be against Trump, but if you agree with him on anything – anything at all – liberals will label you racist or sexist.

You can be against Hillary Clinton, but if you agree with her on anything – anything at all – conservative nuts will label you a communist.

The people who place such labels are not the media. They're bored and inactive people who judge other human beings too much.

The problem with political homers is that each side swears that the other side is filled with ridiculous, ignorant lunatics who are seeking to destroy this country. What they fail to realize is that it's very difficult for the world's leading country to be destroyed by any one group of people... but the country does have a minuscule chance of being destroyed only because of the inability to listen to each other's ideas and perspectives respectfully.

People don't understand that by suppressing the speech of those who don't think like them, they're engaging in the very same hatred and discrimination that they claim to be fighting against.

We must listen to those who disagree, care for the bonds that join us together, and find ways to build a society where we all can flourish – even the people who don't look like us, think like us, or vote with us.

Disagreeing with someone shouldn't mean that you don't listen to what they say. That would only make you blinder to other points of view.

If you can't respect other views, then the people with those views will never respect you. This is why we have a country where no Administration or lawmaker can lead effectively... because half the nation refuses to show respect for the offices.

I have friends who are Clinton / Democrat supporters, Trump / Republican supporters, and everything in-between. If they are good people, I respect them. I don't define my friendship with them based on politics, and I learn a great deal from hearing perspectives that differ from my own.

If people can't do this, then they're part of the problem. They are also losers with no true friends.

I don't care if you voted for Trump or Hillary. I don't care if you voted or didn't vote (I didn't).

I don't care if you smoke weed or not. I don't care if you're a drug addict.

I don't care who you marry. I don't care who you hook up with. I don't care how you interpret the legal definition of sexual assault.

I don't care if you want a gun... or 100 guns... or semi-automatic guns... or zero guns.

I don't care if you eat meat. I don't care if you're a vegan (I pretty much am). I don't care if you don't eat chocolate... or if you eat your boogers.

I don't care if you're a (blind) liberal. I don't care if you're a (blind) conservative.

I don't care if you're behind #BlackLivesMatter, #BlueLivesMatter, #AllLivesMatter, or #NoLivesMatterOnSocialMediaBecauseIt's AllBullshit.

None of these things will cause me so much pain and discomfort that I will judge, hold a grudge against, unfriend, or *BLOCK* you on Facebook.

Left-wingers are more intolerant than any other *mainstream* political ideology. This concept is covered in a bestselling book written by psychiatrist Dr. Lyle Rossiter called <u>THE LIBERAL MIND: THE PSYCHOLOGICAL CAUSES OF POLITICAL MADNESS</u>. On social media, digital liberals have no problem name-calling or unfriending on Facebook as their defense.

Another example: during the massive August 2017 Houston floods, University of Tampa Professor Ken Storey tweeted that Hurricane Harvey's destruction was "instant karma" for Texas because it voted Republican and then suggested that Texans deserved the fallout from Hurricane Harvey because of their support for Donald Trump in the 2016 election. After tweeting that "hopefully this will help them realize the GOP doesnt care about them," he clarified that he was "only blaming those who support the GOP," insisting that they need to "do more to stop the evil their state pushes."

How does this scenario not justify the definition of a mental illness?

Storey was fired the next day.

It's tough going against hate-filled digital liberals, and that's what I am doing through this book. Digital liberals have few facts. They have few arguments. But they have very deep emotional psychologies and vocabularies of insults.

For example, I saw an exchange on Facebook that went along the lines of this:

>Honest question: *How many genders are there?*
>Man gives an honest answer: *Two – male and female.*
>Liberals – the People of Tolerance – instantly pile onto man with increasing snark and derision.

This is why division widens. This is why Donald Trump is President. This is why things are the way they are.

You might as well talk to a cinderblock than talk to digital liberals. At least the cinderblock won't call you names.

I'm not saying non-liberals are haters too. Many of them are... so it's a battle of hate.

No political opinion – or facts – has ever changed anyone's mind.

"You're right. I'm changing my vote," said nobody ever.

This book is one big disagreement, and that's OK.

Chapter 1

WHAT IS A DIGITAL LIBERAL?

Digital liberal — a self-proclaimed 'liberal' who stands up for Democratic values on the Internet, social media and other digital platforms but lives a completely different lifestyle of intolerance and close-mindedness to other people, behaviors, opinions and values —
<u>TRUMPBOOK</u>, Naresh Vissa. 2017.

Bill Clinton showed us in the late 1990's that watching or following politics is not meant to be a family spectacle...

The digital liberals must be wondering why they have and continue to put a "racist," "xenophobe," and "conman" on a pedestal. "Vulgar," "sexist," "criminal," "rapist": the words digital liberals apply to President Donald Trump.

Digital liberals made Trump talk... and in that process, they didn't notice his efforts to rally a very large segment of the country behind him. Digital liberals were too busy noticing stuff that didn't matter — like labeling him as "disgusting" for wooing and marrying a supermodel.

Trump was used as a boarding pass just so the digital liberal world could be safer for a few months... or just so liberal mainstream media could take off, as reported by the Hollywood Reporter.

When Trump takes to Twitter or any microphone, the digital liberals read and watch. It's why his debates with Hillary Clinton were the three most watched debates in history. Fortune reported that advertising CPMs were being sold at Super Bowl rates.

Serial podcastpreneur and real estate investor Jason Hartman introduced me to a term called virtue signaling. As cited by *Urban Dictionary*, virtue signaling is merely, "saying you love or hate something to show off what a virtuous person you are, instead of actually trying to fix the problem."

Complaining about Donald Trump on social media feels good to digital liberals, but it doesn't create any solutions or accomplish anything.

Digital liberals pretend they're such great people, but they don't actually do anything. They don't act. They don't put their money where their mouth is. They just write sh*t on Facebook.

Digital liberals don't mingle with people outside their races, ages, interests or socioeconomic statuses. They resort to the "digital world" to live their lives.

Except for Trump, everyone else is honorable. It's unbelievable.

The problem with close-minded digital liberals is that their digital mouths are always open. Before the Election, I thought anti-Trumpers couldn't be more annoying on social media (as opposed to the silent pro-Trumpers and anti-Hillary campers, who were too afraid to speak up about anything pro-Trump or anti-Hillary).

One year later, I can say I was sorely mistaken...

They could actually get more annoying.

Digital liberals propel songs about "pu*sy" "resting in peace" to the top of the Billboard music charts.

Digital liberals read and watch book after book, movie after movie about sexual bondage, discipline, sadism, masochism and pornography. They are responsible for the FIFTY SHADES OF GREY series selling more than 200 million copies in five years (more than what Harry Potter sold during its first 10 years in circulation).

They've created a multibillion dollar industry around it. They buy Christian Grey whips and ropes so they can use them. They are why 30% of all Internet traffic goes to pornography or other sexual material – greater than Netflix, Amazon, Twitter, CNN and ESPN's traffic combined, according to Pornhub.

Yet they complain when other people have consensual hookups.

They refuse to acknowledge the results of their behavior.

Having been so completely out of touch with their fellow citizens that they failed to predict Trump would win, digital liberals are suddenly gifted with the ability to predict how the next few years will go, enough so to justify a foot-stamping level of righteous indignation?

This is them.

Digital liberals say Trump is "unpopular" and has low approval ratings, yet his party's record (which he has endorsed and is responsible for) is 5-0 in Special Elections since he won in November 2016.

5-0... as in undefeated. Perfect.

Furthermore, on Election Day, polls assumed there would be a Democratic House.

WRONG.

Trump impacted all elections across the country – even the smaller ones.

If that's unpopular, then unpopularity and unapproval ratings rule.

Most polls are fraudulent or fake. They couldn't even predict Trump winning. The Princeton Election Consortium found that 97% of polls had Hillary CRUSHING Trump. It also found that Trump had a 1% chance of winning vs. Hillary. Nate Silver even put his percentage that Trump wins at 28%.

Trump isn't "unpopular." He's UNBEATABLE. The *real* numbers prove it.

Michelle Obama and Hillary Clinton commented, "When they [Trump camp] go low, we go high." Instead, they might as well as have said, "When they go low, we go low too."

Digital liberals can wrap themselves with their so-called morality and virtue.

Trump will carry on with his Tweets and speeches. He will bring it all to digital liberals, and they will continue to consume.

They won't change, and neither will Trump.

Some people are famous for what they do....

Trump is infamous for what he does... and he won't stop.

Chapter 2

WHY VOTING DOESN'T MATTER... AND NEITHER DOES POLITICS IN THE UNITED STATES

Facebook Post:

"Trump is already the worst politician and President ever. He lied to the American people."

I'm a political atheist. I don't take sides, and I know almost nothing about politics. I get political news and analysis from the front desk concierge in my condo complex. He listens to political talk during his overnight shifts. It keeps him awake.

I don't vote anymore. The first time I voted in 2008, it was for a Democrat (Barack Obama). The second time I voted, it was for a Republican in 2012 (Mitt Romney).

In 2016, I didn't vote. The people against "fill-in-the-blank" shaming (i.e. body shaming, fat shaming, slut shaming) – by and large digital liberals – went in hard on "vote shaming" third-party voters and non-voters like me. *Politico* interviewed and did a story on me and my reasons for not voting. It was the most read article for them on the day it was published. I had friends call and talk to me for hours criticizing me for not voting.

My response: "OK, if you really want me to vote, I'll vote for Trump next time." And then they'd go ballistic and tell me to stay at home and never vote again.

***

The first life transformation I made was in first grade. I performed very poorly on an admissions test for one of the best private schools in Houston.

The principal gave me a second chance because my parents begged her to... so I was forced to amend my work and study habits. I had to do extra work in addition to all my homework. It was the only way to beat my competition, stand out, and get what my parents and I wanted.

I sought to pay more attention to detail... like clearly distinguishing between the addition (+) and subtraction (-) signs. I followed a daily schedule and put in the hours to improve my math and test-taking skills.

I got into the school. HOORAY!

In 5th grade, I made my second major life transformation.

You see, up until 5th grade, I only had two friends. People called us the Three Musketeers. We were all Indian. We wreaked havoc together.

So people hated us.

I didn't like to be hated. I still don't like to be hated.

At the start of the second semester after Winter Break, I decided I needed a transformation. So I made a decision that would forever change the course of my social life...

I sat at another lunch table with brand new classmates. No more Three Musketeers... it was time to branch out and make new friends. I wanted to be loved.

I was nervous at first.

Will these people like me? Or will they make fun of me?

My fears never materialized. I became friends with everyone at the table. They liked me. Some loved me.

"I'm so happy you're not a Musketeer anymore," a few said. I saw the light.

I loved that they loved me. I felt loved. I loved myself.

So I ran for Student Council. Only two people from my class could be elected. At least 15 people ran.

We care about our own opinions more than other people's, yet we chase other people's approvals constantly.

Like all great politicians, I ran on a platform of promises.

LOWER TUITION!

NEW GYM!

START A FOOTBALL TEAM!

Oh, and the most important issue students from private schools faced: what they ate...

NEW LUNCH MENUS!

OPEN MCDONALD'S IN THE CAFETERIA!

And like all the great politicians, I came up with a slogan that was sure to sway the masses:

DO YOU SMELL WHAT NARESH IS COOKING?

No better way to bring change to the food we ate than to steal a line from the most popular entertainer at the time (1999/2000): The Rock (the wrestler turned Hollywood actor Dwayne Johnson), who's theme song started with, "Do you smell what The Rock is cooking?"

On my campaign posters, I included testimonials from The Rock and Uncle Sam. I had no idea who Uncle Sam was, but my campaign advisor two grades above me told me to use him. He was already a Student Council member, and I was trying to get him to pull strings for me.

I made my parents spend a few hundred dollars on campaign badges. The badges said, "Vote 4 Naresh." What a waste of money! Sorry mom and dad... dinner is on me next time!

My dad helped me write a speech. It was very formal. There were many big words in there that I didn't know and couldn't pronounce... like "brethren" and "cohort" and "constituency" and "marked."

And then at the end of the speech, I ignored the formalities and ended loudly with:

"So Vote For Naresh!... IF YOU SMELLLLLLLLLLLLLLLL... WHAT NARESH!... IS COOKING!!!"

MIC DROP

And then the girls laughed at me and said things like, "What a weirdo, I'm not voting for him," while the guys said, "That was awesome!"

My dad didn't want me to do that, but that's all I wanted to do. It was actually the reason why I was running... because it was the only chance I had in my young life where everyone would be watching and listening to what I had to say. I wanted it to be memorable.

***

The day before voting, a scandal erupted. One of the leading female candidates issued an apology to the class because she lied. She said she submitted lyrics to the manager of the popular boy band *NSYNC and that they used her lyrics to make a song in their hit album NO STRINGS ATTACHED. She brought the letter *NSYNC wrote to thank her for her work. It was signed by all the members.

She garnered support from the entire school... not just our grade. Teachers were proud. She was giving speeches to all the classes. She became a school celebrity.

It turned out it was all a sham. She wrote the letter herself and forged the signatures.

THE THINGS PEOPLE DO TO BE ELECTED!

Voting happened the next morning. Each student had two votes for two open positions.

I voted for myself, even though I told people I didn't. I told every other candidate that I voted for him or her, thinking they would vote for me back. If I got enough competitors to vote for me with their second vote, then I shouldn't have had a problem getting one of the two elected positions.

***

The night before results were announced, I couldn't sleep... not because I was worried about delivering on my promises, but because I wanted to win! I wanted to be on the Student Council and have all the power! I wanted my classmates to bow down to me and treat me the way I deserved to be treated (*Naresh* means "King of kings" in Sanskrit).

When I showed up to school the next morning, the results were posted on the hallway. I didn't even have to check them. My classmates were already yelling the winners. My friends told me I lost with big smiles on their faces.

Their smiles made me feel better. I smiled but was still sad.

I made a mistake with my campaign strategy. I didn't consider the disparity between boys and girls. The girls outnumbered the boys about nearly 2:1 in our class... which meant whomever got the female vote won.

This was 5th grade, when boys still played with boys on the playground, and girls still played with girls. Both sexes were close to making a full recovery from cooties, but not quite yet. There was a little bit of interaction between the two sexes, but it was subtle in the form of AOL Instant Messenger and flirtatious love notes being passed around in the middle of class.

Two girls won the election. Go figure.

Running on a platform based on The Rock and food probably wasn't the brightest idea.

"You can always try again next year," my mother said. So I did. And I lost again.

I felt like Ross Perot. He was a laughingstock politician in Texas, which is where I grew up.

But then I won the year after that! I had the most boring campaign. No badges, no promises, no crazy speeches. I put in very little effort. And I won!

***

What did I do once I was elected as a Representative to the Student Council?

Absolutely nothing.

I showed up to the meetings and said, "Here," during roll call. I ate my lunch diligently (the meetings were held during lunch). I voted on things I had no clue about. I dicked around with my friends from the basketball team who were also elected.

I realized how much of an act this entire process was. Outside of putting on a middle school dance, there was no progress or changes being made. The food stayed the same. Tuition has risen by more than 300% ever since. It wasn't until the school was bought by an education management company that a new gym was built and football team was created.

The elected Student Councilmen and women did nothing outside of toot their horns, command respect, and write down their positions on resumes for high school applications.

***

In the United States of America, none of these political charades matter. They are weapons of mass distraction – political WMDs.

That's a good thing... because we're not an African or Middle Eastern nation ruling with Sharia Law, where women have their clits removed, are stoned or executed if they look at other men, can't drive, or can't be educated. Relatively speaking, men have limited freedoms in these places too.

No system is perfect. There is always room for tweaking and improvement.

Nevertheless, I don't see the issues and weaknesses in the U.S. system that other people see...

In 2012, when I was much more politically active as a voter, I criticized the system for letting dumb, uneducated, illiterate people vote because then Romney would have no chance at winning. Most of them voted for Obama.

I now realize that I was wrong. Those people need voices too. The system allows them to be a part of the political process. That's a staple of our country and democracy.

This country is not a person. It's a complex system made up of trillions of moving parts. One person can't affect change on a massive scale. That's not how democracy is set up.

Under the U.S. system, electing a Saddam Hussein or Adolf Hitler would be nearly impossible. Furthermore, checks and balances prevent a Saddam Hussein or Adolf Hitler (if they were miraculously elected) from exerting their power and taking over the country single-handedly. It's not just the federal government that has power, but the states, municipalities, towns, and counties too. Nobody can ever get so powerful to violate human rights egregiously.

Case in point: A week after President Donald Trump's 2017 inauguration, he issued an Executive Order to ban immigrants from seven countries – Iran, Libya, Somalia, Syria, Iraq, Sudan, and Yemen – from entering the United States. The immigration ban was fully active for a day before a lawsuit was filed and green card holders were allowed in. Then, the ban was active for a few more days until judges in various states ruled the Executive Order unconstitutional, at which point, everything went back to normal.

So while the Executive Order made for tense news headlines and water cooler talk, "the system" kept the process in check and kept things from getting out of hand.

If a President abuses the law, then he can be impeached by Congress or voted out within four years. Four years is a very short amount of time in the political process.

The President only has one power under the *Constitution* anyway, and that is to make treaties, which are rarely negotiated in today's geopolitical landscape.

Note: the President CANNOT WAGE WAR unilaterally under the *Constitution*. The House of Representatives (part of Congress) has to vote on it and then declare.

When it comes to lawmaking, the current majority Republican Congress (Senate and House of Representatives) and Republican Supreme Court has been dictating policy more than Trump. This makes his job far easier to the point that he can take extra vacation days to golf.

The President can have opinions. He can recommend ideas... like creating the Department of Education (Jimmy Carter), which, since its creation, the U.S. has gone from #1 in the world in education to #18... or he can recommend that Fannie Mae reduce their lending standards so that more people can afford homes (Bill Clinton and George W. Bush) – eventually causing the housing bust and 2008 financial crisis.

In fact, I'd bring up the idea of not even having a President and just letting the legislative and judicial branches run the federal government. The states, municipalities and counties can run the rest of the governments.

It's so important that kids in America be taught about the way the U.S. government works and operates in social studies, civics and government courses at an early age. That way, when kids grow up to live in the real world, they understand that the system is set up to *protect* them, not hurt them... so they won't need to waste their time or energy on politics or blaming the government for their shortfalls. As they grow older, and they see the harsh systems and events taking place in other countries, they will appreciate what they have here. The U.S. government is designed and run for the people, so it should be supported as long as it continues to exist in this sense.

Our politicians don't go around in tanks shooting civilians (like in many other nations). The Federal Reserve is in place to keep the economy and the dollar as a currency in check (in addition to deflation, which has always been more of a threat to the U.S. than inflation).

The administrators at my school when I was younger were part of their own checks and balances academic system. They were the ones who really made shit happen. We student council reps could say or *try* to do whatever we wanted... but at the end of the day, school officials made the rational decisions. They made sure crazy little 13-year-olds wouldn't bring the school down.

***

People who say they'll move out of the country if Candidate X is elected... where will they go?

Singapore, which is one of the most expensive countries in the world? Good luck affording that.

Australia, New Zealand, Ireland, Switzerland, Germany, Japan, Russia, UK, France? Same case.

You could move to a cheaper country like Argentina, Colombia, Thailand, Indonesia or India... but I wish you all the best in finding a job that will pay you well for your qualifications... and best of luck finding a quality of life and standard of living that lives up to the U.S.

We're still under a bipartisan system... so progress happens slowly. But when "change" happens, it's for the better. And if it's not, it's only a matter of one or two terms (4-8 years) for the "change" to be overturned – again, for the better of the greatest number of citizens.

I'd much rather live in a political system like this than one that can go from capitalist to communist or dictatorial overnight, like so many authoritarian states like Egypt, Syria and Libya.

***

Think about the highest and lowest points of your life. Write them down. Here are just a few of mine that come to mind:

HIGH:

- Being born to my parents
- Getting into and graduating college and grad school
- Getting an amazing job out of school
- Celebrating special events with friends and family

LOW:

- Being demoted or failing classes
- Being impeached and removed as President of my class in high school
- Terrible things that happened to people close to me throughout my life
- Being fired multiple times
- Girls breaking up with me
- Houston Rockets losing in the NBA Playoffs the one year I had season tickets and went to 45 home games
- Deaths

NOT A SINGLE THING I MENTIONED HAD ANYTHING TO DO WITH WHO WAS PRESIDENT, GOVERNOR, MAYOR, ETC. I've lived in cities where I didn't even know who the elected officials were. I have no idea who my current Congressman or Congresswoman is. I don't know what District I live in. I don't know who's running Tampa City Hall.

Fervent political supporters may say, "Well, that's selfish of you to say because then the poor will be screwed if a right-wing radical is elected [or insert any issue here]." The poor will always get their entitlements... even if Ron Paul (fiscal right-winger) was President. The system is set up that way. The U.S. will never let poor people take over a country. It will never degrade itself to Third World status or even an India with such a large discrepancy between the haves and have-nots. The U.S. is not a country ruled by *one person*, but rather a country ruled by tens of thousands of pieces that are at play. 99% of these people are college-educated with top 1% backgrounds and qualifications.

Was Thomas Jefferson a good President? Many of you will say yes because he's a Founding Father and there are statues of him around the country.

The *New York Daily News* reported that he had a fetish for raping slaves.

Was Woodrow Wilson a good President? He cruised the U.S. to victory during World War I.

The Atlantic reports he was a supporter of the Ku Klux Klan.

Was FDR a good President? He suffered from polio and was bound to a wheelchair for most of his life, yet he had tremendous courage in leading the United States to victory in World War II.

He also turned away German Jews from immigrating to the U.S. while they were being exterminated in their home country, and he also put Japanese immigrants and U.S. citizens of Japanese ancestry in internment camps.

Was Ronald Reagan a good President? His supply-side Reaganomics is credited with the dot-com boom and creation of the online and digital workforce and economy.

His son said he had Alzheimer's while in office and never told the public.

Was Bill Clinton a good President? Many people believe he was responsible for the 90's economic boom.

The Washington Post reported that he stuck a cigar up his intern's tw*t and sucked on it while in the Oval Office. AMAZING FEAT FOR A PRESIDENT TO PULL OFF!

Donald Trump is racist. Hillary Clinton is communist and hides secret emails.

We all have skeletons.

***

Most people (including me) don't know much about politics outside of the headlines.

Let's play a game to prove this point further...

It is time to elect a world leader, and your vote counts. Here are the facts about the three leading candidates:

Candidate A: Associates with crooked politicians and consults with astrologers... he's had two mistresses. He also chain-smokes and drinks 8 to 10 martinis a day.

Candidate B: He was kicked out of office twice, sleeps until noon, used opium in college, and drinks a quart of whiskey every evening.

Candidate C: He is a decorated war hero. He's a vegetarian, doesn't smoke, drinks an occasional beer, and hasn't had any extramarital affairs.

Which of these candidates would be your choice?

TAKE SOME TIME TO THINK ABOUT IT...

TAKE SOME TIME TO THINK ABOUT IT...

I vote for C. 92% of the people I've given this quiz to have also.

Here are the results:

Candidate A is Franklin D. Roosevelt.

Candidate B is Winston Churchill.

Candidate C is Adolf Hitler.

So... what makes a leader a good leader?

Nothing...

As a voter, there is no science to knowing the answer to this question no matter how brilliant you are.

There is no perfect person. We all have our problems.

Candidate C (Hitler) led a genocide AFTER he was elected... NOT BEFORE. How were the voters supposed to know? How were his subordinates (many of them Jewish) who supported him supposed to know?

That's why YOUR VOTE DOESN'T COUNT.

The idea that your vote counts and will change anyone's life drastically is an outright lie. No political candidate will ever care about you or the people. It's always about them. They *say* anything to get themselves elected... because they're politicians. They're narcissists, deceivers and power hungry. It's the only way they can be elected... because voters are that irrational.

Democracy is the process of appealing to the unsophisticated masses who can't distinguish between entertainment and politics. Donald Trump is a show businessman, and politics is show business for ugly people.

Our officials are nothing more than actors playing roles of elected representatives on news programs. Once the cameras are off, they focus their primary duties on advocating for multinational corporations at all costs — including the health and wealth of people.

The illusion of beneficial and effective government is created by the mainstream media and the architecturally sound buildings and monuments in Washington D.C. and City Halls across the country. Government is nothing more than scripted fiction... an illusion for the naive.

Politicians are professional liars. It's impossible to make it so far as to be called a politician without lying. It's why I don't vote or idolize any of these narcissists.

President Donald Trump conned the rest of the world into buying his "plan" – which consisted of nothing...

But which successful politicians aren't cons?

In this country, the cons and liars win elections.

Think about the politicians you personally know: former classmates who strive to get on Boards, friends who constantly self-promote on Facebook, people you know who must be in the spotlight.

Do you trust these people? Would you make them your child's godparents or partner with them in business?

These people are the politicians who run for office or will run for exalted positions in the future, and they will continue to fool people... just like that classmate of mine fooled an entire school into thinking she wrote a song for *NSYNC.

In graduate school at Duke, there was someone in our class who ran for a club president, and he promised all these great things so people would vote for him. He won in a landslide, but then resigned a few months after he got what he needed from the position (a top job).

That's politics.

In Trump's case, he has already toned down his rhetoric in his first year as President. Mexico isn't planning to pay for the Wall, Hillary won't be investigated or prosecuted, and Obamacare hasn't been completely repealed – all broken promises.

That's politics again... and it should make digital liberals and Trump haters happy.

But it's still important to give Trump a chance because what he will do will be very different from what he said to be relevant as a dark horse candidate to gain votes. It's quite incredible what Trump accomplished when the odds were stacked against him from day one all the way until the evening of Election Day.

I voted in 2008 because it was the first time I was old enough to vote. I remember the feeling. I thought I was doing a great service to the country. It gave me a lot of confidence.

But two years later, I realized the guy I voted for (Barack Obama) lied...

He said he would crack down on Wall Street following the Great Recession that was created by our financial institutions. Instead, he bailed them out and raised tens of millions of dollars from them when he was running for re-election in 2012, according to the *Wall Street Journal.*

He said he would initiate military strikes in pockets of Pakistan to fight terrorism. That didn't happen. The War against Terrorism got worse under Obama – not better...

ISIS wasn't around in 2008 when Obama was elected. ISIS had little support in 2012 when he was re-elected. Al-Qaeda and Taliban are still hanging out in Pakistan.

There are a million other things I could say about his lies and any other political type of figure.

Anyone who believes any word coming out of a politician's mouth is naive enough to be deservedly conned.

That's why it's so important to look at what people *do* rather than what they *say*. *What* you do is much more important than *what you say*.

People's actions should speak so loudly that nobody can hear what they're saying.

If you don't do (new) things, you don't get experience.

Going to work and performing the same function every day for 20 years is not experience.

Having sex in the same position with the same woman is not experience.

Thinking is not experience.

DOING THINGS is experience.

Politicians rarely do what they *say* they're going to do. The public is starting to take notice, which is why the Ipsos MORI Veracity Index found politicians to be some of the least trusted people in society today. The recent Election of 2016 took public distrust in the media and status quo politics mainstream.

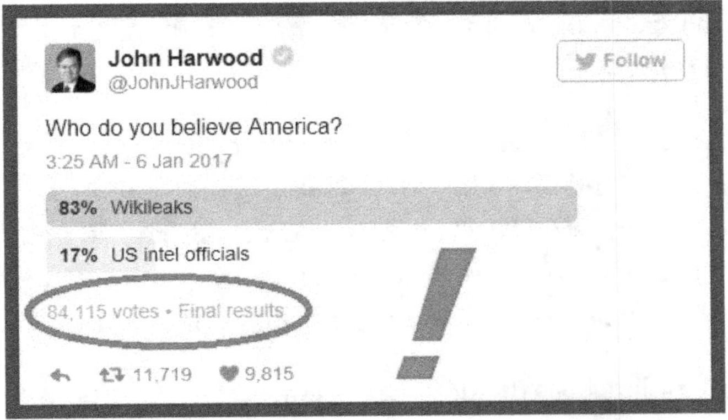

Only one in six Americans can be taken for fools.

If you ever want to be cheated by a politician, just tell him or her you love them unconditionally. They'll then consistently screw and neglect you the entire time they're in office.

I choose to stop validating corruption by participating in the voting process.

Money talks, and bullshit walks.

***

Facebook Post:

"Being a great leader is being a unifying force, not a divisive one."

Ideal leaders are peaceful unifiers like Mahatma Gandhi and Martin Luther King... but these types of people don't run for political office because they don't win elections.

Margaret Thatcher, FDR, Alexander the Great, Julius Caesar, Indira Gandhi, Narendra Modi, Teddy Roosevelt, and Abraham Lincoln are all considered to be some of our greatest leaders... but these were all some of the most divisive figures in human history.

In politics, "divide and conquer" works. The longstanding theory of "divide and conquer" has been the oldest Machiavellian political tactic since the cavemen, even before Machiavelli theorized it himself as a strategy in <u>THE PRINCE</u>. Divide and conquer has been the eternal political policy since the Greek, Roman, and British empires to modern-day politics. Alexander the Great did it. Genghis Khan, the Moghul Dynasty, and Caesar did it. Reagan, FDR, Bush, Obama all did it. Hillary Clinton did it too... she just didn't do it well enough. It's why Adolph Hitler had a shot at taking over the world. He was the closest to doing so post-status quo antebellum. It's the oldest Machiavellian strategy to gain control and power. In recent memory, nobody in this country has done it as explicitly as Trump though. The US has been a divided nation since Thomas Jefferson and the advent of bipartisanship.

If you don't want to divide people, then don't run for political office. You won't win.

Hillary and Trump were divisive. Obama was divisive. Bush was divisive. Bill Clinton, Reagan, Nixon... all divisive. You don't win anything without being divisive. It's why Kerry, McCain, and Romney lost in 2004, 2008 and 2012. They weren't divisive enough.

The 2016 GOP nomination was planned for Jeb Bush or Marco Rubio per leaked WikiLeaks e-mails. Why didn't either come close to winning? Because people didn't vote for them... they weren't divisive enough. They voted for Donald Trump instead — the most divisive candidate of the bunch.

Trump has no hesitation whatsoever to act with an iron fist. Kerry, McCain, Jeb Bush, Rubio and Romney tried to please everyone, which doesn't work in politics.

Is it right? Probably not... but that's the way it is, and the way it will always be.

It's not about policy or the issues. They don't matter. Trump wouldn't have made it out of the primaries if he only discussed the issues and his policies toward them. That's why all the other Republicans performed so poorly. It's why Trump got nowhere when he ran in 2000 as a Reform candidate. There were few criticisms of him. Most people loved him when he was on *The Apprentice*.

The most hated people will always come out on top. Most times, the most loved person happens to also be the most hated person.

Haters are typically a sign of success for those being hated. The hard work of those being hated on reminds people of their own inadequacies, and that's why they are constantly hated on, lashed out at, or criticized.

If you want everyone to love you, just be a big failure or loser. People will feel sorry for you and never consider you to be a threatening competitor.

***

There are thousands of political issues to address. Just as nobody's perfect, so too there is no perfect candidate. Criticizing a politician for *one thing* he or she says or believes is myopic. For every issue you disagree with a candidate, there are millions of other people who support it.

There is no perfect family. We don't have perfect parents. We don't get married to a perfect spouse, nor do we have perfect kids.

We are not perfect.

Complaints start and never stop – with ourselves too.

Political people act like they have all the solutions. If that's the case, then they should fix every problem in the world. They should run for office. Instead, they piss off just as many people.

Trump haters think a certain way, but geniuses like billionaire techpreneur Peter Thiel think a completely different way... a way that supports Trump.

There are always multiple sides to any given issue. For every reason Democrats give on raising taxes, multiple leading PhD scholars can counter with an equally compelling argument on why lowering taxes would prove to be more beneficial.

At the end of the day, who's right?

Nobody is. We all just have to accept each other and the way things play out.

There is no science to resolving the issues.

Voting is acting on an opinion. Everyone is entitled to a vote just like everyone is entitled to an opinion...

But a non-voter like me tries to see two sides to the coin and just accepts things as they are. Everyone is right, and everyone is wrong. Politics shouldn't be an issue in the reality of a voter's life.

People have the right to vote. Who are we to tell them not to? I choose to stay at home because voting is a waste of time... but I have that right too.

Life is too short to waste time on fighting over political issues that have no solutions. It's OK to ignore nonsense and bullsh*t. Nonsense and bullsh*t are always distractions.

***

Too many naïve and desperate people depend on one candidate winning. Why? Because they think this candidate can save them and their situations...

I once dated a woman who put off her studies because she truly believed a left-wing socialist with a lowercase "s" (Bernie Sanders) would become President. She thought he would get her debt and student loans to disappear. She also thought she'd get more entitlements from the government.

So she quit graduate school...

For months, she justified that Bernie would become President... even when he was being slaughtered in the primaries and polls by Hillary Clinton AND Donald Trump. Sanders stayed in the Democratic race because the Democratic Party wouldn't let him quit. It's like the worst teams in professionals sports playing out the second half of a season even though everyone knows they're so bad that they have no shot in God's name of making the Playoffs.

It wasn't until Sanders conceded that my friend accepted he lost... and she was devastated when that happened – like crying on the floor devastated.

She complained about it nonstop...

"This country is stupid!"

"Bernie is so generous! He'd make the country nicer!!!"

This is the problem with people who put their lives into any one candidate... or any other person or thing for that matter...

Don't ever believe people can only progress with government help. You can keep waiting for the government to save you... or you can find your own ways to help yourself and improve your situation instead of sitting around hoping some quacks in D.C. will come around.

People shouldn't be putting their faith in the government. That is a recipe for disaster.

People should be putting more faith in themselves.

It's your job to succeed regardless of what CNN is feeding you or who's President.

We have to prepare for the chaos that lies in front of us. It's a jungle out there, and no political party or politician will ever save you. You must find a way to save yourself.

Don't ever give your control to anyone or anything – even God.

Don't ever let anyone or anything else take control of your life!

Unless you're a billionaire who wants to become a trillionaire because of some complex offshore tax loopholes, then no politician can save (or really help) you.

Want to be considerate to others? Simple...

Volunteer... write checks... tip whoever you want... fundraise... create organizations that help others... offer your time...

But do not expect to outsource generosity to a middleman – like any government.

Generosity comes from within.

Not everyone can get their way all the time. If you expect to go through life by getting everything you want, then you'll eventually be diagnosed with depression and crying on the floor like the woman I mentioned. The world will break your heart if you think it's going to treat you fairly or if you think your personal, subjective definition of "good" or "right" will prevail over "evil" or "wrong" all the time.

I don't get the hurt people feel when it comes to U.S. politics. It's not a funeral for a loved one.

Explaining U.S. politics would involve a deeper discussion on constitutional law, the checks and balances system, impeachment processes, term limits, federal vs. state vs. municipal vs. county governments, and the democratic society we live in.

Politics has been a complete mystery to me since I started hearing about it during the Election of 1996. I will never understand why people are so vested in such charades, just like I don't understand why people get so vested in their sports teams.

Politics and politicians are not crystal balls. None of us have real crystal balls that tell us how we're going to feel in the future or what's going to happen to us. Fear and worry about politics or proverbial crystal balls are not good ways to live life.

That's why anyone who believes any word coming out of a politician's mouth is naive enough to be deservedly conned.

***

Less than 10 years after I was finally elected for Student Council, I started my first service business.

So I became a businessman... not a politician. I'm still a businessman today. I've started (and shut down) multiple businesses. I've made and lost. I've hired and fired.

Overall, it's been great.

I will also continue to live my life the way I've been living it. I'll strive to grow my businesses. I'll continue to publish my books. I'll love my family and friends. I'll play tennis, beach volleyball, basketball and chess.

It's important people focus on themselves and what's most important in their lives. For example, two-time NBA MVP and champion Stephen Curry and four-time NBA MVP and three-time champion Lebron James delete all their social media apps from their phones during the Playoffs.

"When you're really trying to zone in and keep your focus, you don't want to have any unnecessary distractions," Curry told ESPN. "We have goals to accomplish, and you want to make sure you're giving your all."

Here are two successful human beings who admit to shutting down media and other distractions so they can better succeed at their crafts and in life.

Give politicians respect they deserve, but never worship them. When you put people on a pedestal and portray them as superhuman, it separates you from your own greatest potential.

Don't just remain an extreme admirer or a bystander. Jump in and relish in your own extraordinary capability.

When people say anything about our public politicians, some of us get our feelings hurt or feel the need to throw hissy fits, particularly on social media. I feel sad for such people who worship politicians or the government – whether through love or hate – rather than celebrating the greatness and potential that lies within them. Such people are better off spending their time and mindshare being better workers, citizens, students, investors, and business owners than arguing with their inner social circles about the definition of racism or assault on Facebook.

If people spent as much time learning to improve themselves to succeed as they spend reading ephemeral news or following and arguing meaningless political developments that are out of our hands, we would be far ahead in our lives and for future generations to come. In other words, people could get a lot further in life if they spent less time being emotional and more time worrying about themselves. Unfortunately, people choose to escape from reality and get caught up in inapt charades, and that's why the world has always been so divided.

If you don't improve yourself, you end up arguing politics on Facebook and disappear into the normalcy of your life.

Some people are so lazy and myopic that they must have their minds controlled, be fed corporate propaganda, and have information hidden from them. For example, a radio producer told me that a station told him that he COULD NOT mention Bernie Sanders on the air.

Unfortunately, there are people who feel so threatened by freedom of thought and information that they would rather be lied to, manipulated, managed like sheep and told what to do.

People tend to be obsessed with entertainment, sports, politics, superficiality and drama, while not nearly as enthusiastic about learning, training, preparation and building. They spend more time talking about the news, random monuments and statues after they're taken down, a fight, a football game, a TV show or a concert than they spend talking about educating their kids or building their family business. This is where people open themselves up to the attacks they experience.

The solution for all this political nonsense is for people to build wealth and long-lasting relationships for the next generation so our children can compete against the Trumps and Clintons of the world with more than just marches, rallies, #hashtags and prayer vigils.

Choose yourself and those around you – not the President. It doesn't matter who the President is. What matters is who you surround yourself with. Only you and those around you can make a real impact on your life.

Donald Trump is not a billionaire President of the United States of America because of his political policies or wealth. There are hundreds of politically astute veterans and billionaires who can't in their right mind imagine getting the keys to one of the most powerful positions in the world.

Trump is President because 80 years ago, his father Fred Trump planted seeds that allowed The Donald to have the wealth and power necessary to become one of the leaders of New York City and eventually the free world...

You see, Fred Trump started as a laborer and built a BUSINESS that created an economic empire he was able to pass on to his children. This allowed them to start the professional game of adulthood with head starts.

While other 25-year-olds were trying to find their first jobs, Donald Trump was the CEO of a multimillion dollar company. Yes, this was handed to him by his father, but The Donald learned how to lead large masses of people who depended on his success for their own livelihoods.

Fred didn't just throw The Donald into the firepits. He implicitly TAUGHT his son about wealth at an early age and prepared him to win at a rigged American economic game. He sent him to the Wharton School at the Ivy League's University of Pennsylvania to study finance and economics and drilled in him how to win in business – or at least how to remain competitive. While we might want to challenge Trump's faulty ethics, he is a tough person who played a very dirty game on his way to the top.

Fred also instilled DISCIPLINE in The Donald. That sounds crazy to digital liberals given The Donald's undisciplined Tweets at random hours of the night, but understand that at an early age, Fred sent The Donald to a military academy where he learned the art of warfare. Kids aren't sent to military academies for fun unless their parents encourage them. This militaristic discipline played a role in The Donald's ability to sustain himself during relentless attacks from the Left, digital liberals, and the mainstream news media.

The Donald also learned there is no winning if you spend the bulk of your time whining. It takes discipline, vision, execution and hard work to accomplish success.

The knowledge, investment and discipline Fred taught The Donald allowed The Donald to become the leader of the free world.

The Donald's life story and rise to Presidency is a great way to raise children to become economic champions and polymaths.

Donald Trump doesn't care if you like him or not. As much as digital liberals want to fight, moan, scream and yell to the rooftops, The Donald was able to get what he wanted because his father planted seeds nearly a century ago that paved the path for his children and grandchildren to become economic and political champions.

The Election of 2016 was not won in 2016. It was won in 1936.

No matter what anyone thinks about you or how few friends you have, our children should be able to gain the ability to shape their own destiny and not feel like they've been pushed to the sidelines by their own parents.

It's not what you leave for your children. It's what you leave in your children.

What will your children and grandchildren be able to do in 80 years because of what you're doing today?

I sure as hell know whining and complaining about politicians on social media won't do anything for anyone.

Politicians don't bring change. Innovation and our OWN personal impacts on the world will have far greater effect than any President. Political elections are just a game.

Outside of ourselves, the real change is happening in 3D printing, artificial intelligence, virtual reality and technological innovation in various facets of our lives.

There is a great deal of opportunity for those who seek it out. Life is very good in the United States right now no matter who is in the White House. For example, the standard of living for a poor person in the United States – A/C housing, smartphones, EBT cards, food stamps, Medicaid, etc. – is far greater than the rich in many countries.

Be bold and move forward. Don't be a cog, and don't be afraid.

***

I won't be voting again unless a fellow close friend who is also Hindu runs. I'm a Brown Indian Hindu Nationalist / Supremacist. I want India, Indians and Indo-Americans to do well.

I'm a believer in democracy. I want what the people in a given system want. Voters can do the work for me. Whether it's a Republican or Democrat, I will support it.

We live in a wonderful nation, and no one person can take away our freedoms and liberties!

Saying it's your "civic duty" to vote is not accurate or realistic. There is no rule or law that says you have to vote or else you will lose your citizenship or die.

As human beings, we have civil responsibilities – but voting is not one of them...

I have civil responsibilities like running my businesses, offering great products and services, hiring people to work for me and paying them, writing books and publishing other content, mentoring the next set of fervent youngsters, loving my friends and family, eating and living healthy, and donating my time, money and blood (I'm a frequent blood donor) to charities.

You too can decide how to fulfill your civil responsibilities. If you choose voting, watching television news, and posting on social media, then that's fine. Go right ahead. Who am I to stop you?

But I choose not to do that, and that's a right I have. My desire to build myself, my family / friends, my businesses, and those around me makes me incapable of waking up and complaining about Donald Trump all day.

Your civil duty isn't to vote. Your duty is to succeed no matter who wins... because change doesn't happen with a vote. Change happens within us, and true change starts with changing ourselves.

For everyone else who disagrees, there's Election Day.

***

If you can keep your head when all about you;
Are losing theirs and blaming it on you,
If you can trust yourself when all men doubt you,
But make allowance for their doubting too.
If you can wait and not be tired by waiting,
Or being lied about, don't deal in lies,
Or being hated, don't give way to hating,
And yet don't look too good, nor talk too wise:

If you can dream—and not make dreams your master;
If you can think—and not make thoughts your aim;
If you can meet with Triumph and Disaster,
And treat those two impostors just the same;
If you can bear to hear the truth you've spoken
Twisted by knaves to make a trap for fools,
Or watch the things you gave your life to, broken,
And stoop and build 'em up with worn-out tools:

If you can make a heap of all your winnings
And risk it on one turn of pitch-and-toss,
And lose, and start again at your beginnings
And never breathe a word about your loss;
If you can force your heart and nerve and sinew
To serve your turn long after they are gone,
And so hold on when there is nothing in you
Except the Will which says to them: "Hold on!"

If you can talk with crowds and keep your virtue,
  Or walk with Kings—nor lose the common touch,
If neither foes nor loving friends can hurt you,
  If all men count with you, but none too much;
If you can fill the unforgiving minute
  With sixty seconds' worth of distance run,
Yours is the Earth and everything that's in it,
  And—which is more—you'll be a Man, my son!

If—
By Rudyard Kipling

Chapter 3

7 REASONS WHY THE NEWS MEDIA IS SCAMMING YOU

I'm allowed to criticize the news and media. Why? Because I've been a member of the media since I was 15.

My involvement in media and publishing has evolved drastically over the years, from reporter, editor, producer and consumer to manager, publisher, entrepreneur and non-consumer.

I graduated from Syracuse University's S.I. Newhouse School of Public Communications – the best journalism school in the country according to *NewsPro* (go Orange!). I dreamed of becoming a sports broadcaster. I reported some incredible stories about race, politics, partying, and strippers.

And then I gave it all up...

I lost faith in the profession. It wasn't about the truth. It was about eyeballs, comments, Retweets, and Likes.

The business models were changing post-2008. Media companies were going bankrupt left and right. Outside of Bloomberg, very few outlets paid their interns. ESPN stopped recruiting from our campus, which was the first ESPNU. Starting salaries were in the $20,000s. Some of my classmates accepted contract work that paid them $10-12 an hour capped at 20 hours a week.

But with the destruction in media and publishing came tremendous opportunity...

During my senior year of college, I did my Honors Capstone thesis on how podcasting was going to boom. This was before most people knew what podcasting was. Four years later, I expanded on my thesis and turned it into a #1 bestselling book, PODCASTNOMICS. I'm still collecting royalties from it.

I helped clients start up and run their podcasts. They didn't need to be hired by radio stations anymore. They could do it all themselves and let their voices be heard in a real, unedited, unplugged and genuine manner.

The status quo and mainstream don't understand that though. Old school corporatists run them.

My professors in college weren't talking about podcasting, online publishing, monetization strategies, or new business models... so when the students started working, they quickly learned that it was about the headline – not the story.

All the news media does is feed you a load of crap... so you can feel good about yourself and share that crap on Facebook so your friends can feel good about themselves too... so you can get scared and share that crap on Facebook so your friends can feel scared too... so you can lie to yourself that you're a more educated person about the world because you read a bunch of words that mean nothing 24-48 hours later.

My full distrust in the media started in my mid-20's when I was working in the publishing industry. I saw firsthand how misleading and hyperbolic headlines and sub-headlines grabbed audiences. I also saw competitors using such strategies to prey on consumers.

We now live in a society where fake news outperforms real news. A *BuzzFeed News* analysis found that top fake election news stories generated more total engagement on Facebook than top election stories from 19 major news outlets combined.

If you want to be a truly powerless person, just keep blindly consuming the mainstream news media that are all owned by FNN: The Fake News Network.

Here's why I refuse to actively read, watch or consume the mainstream media:

1) **The news is the worst driver for investing.**

I had to read the news every day in journalism school. We had current events quizzes frequently in class. In 2010, I read all about the slow death of Europe. It was supposed to spread to Asia and then the United States. The death of Greece was going to bring about a double-dip global recession.

So I shorted the market... I put all the money I earned during a summer internship at a Bulge Bracket bank into these investments.

The investments went straight down. Outside of a spike in August / September 2011 because of a U.S. debt downgrade by some subjective agency (meaning absolutely nothing), economies improved and gold tanked.

Bye-bye internship money...

The best investments have no correlation with the news. They survive and thrive *despite* the news.

So don't read the news... the people writing it have no background in what they're reporting. How many PhDs do you see reporting in any mainstream publication? I like Dr. Sanjay Gupta. He's actually a doctor who covers medicine and health.

The mainstream is over-saturated with a bunch of misinformed and unworldly college graduates who know how to write and conduct interviews but very little about what it all means. That's why the mainstream news media is the "idiot's medium."

2) The people who produce media content know nothing about what they're covering.

The idea of "covering events" and press conferences is 20th century and unnecessary today.

The media is as gullible as its users. Ryan Holiday's book <u>TRUST ME I'M LYING: Confessions of a Media Manipulator</u> goes into detail on how pathetic and negligent the highest national and international level reporters can be. To prove his claim, Holiday duped the media by posing as an expert on random subjects. He bullshitted journalists, and they didn't even bother to fact check him and went ahead with their stories, quoting him as their source!

Mohammed Islam did something similar. Who is Mohammed Islam? A nobody. But why am I referencing him? Because he was featured on CNBC, *Vanity Fair*, the *Christian Science Monitor*, *New York Post*, *International Business Times*, CNN, *New York Magazine*, *The*

Guardian... pretty much every major publication out there.

For what? For making north of $70 million trading stocks as a high school senior...

Five days after his fame hit the news, he hired a PR firm to arrange more interviews... just so he could tell the same publications that covered his successes that he lied about it all and had a net worth of zero.

The mainstream news media proves again it's the "idiot's medium." A recent scientific study conducted by neuroscientist Tara Swift and the London Press Club reported that journalists' brains function at a lower level than the rest of the population. The study concluded that "the highest functions of journalists' brains were operating at a lower level than the average population." In other words, journalists' brains show a lower level of executive function – the ability of the brain to regulate emotions, suppress biases, switch between tasks, solve complex problems and think flexibly and creatively – than the average person.

Journalists are people too. They'll believe – and report on – anything so long as it increases their metrics.

3) The news cycle is limited. Most of what you read will be forgotten.

Whatever is happening in the news won't affect you today or in the future. In early 2014, Ukraine and Russia were fighting in Crimea. I don't know the details because I didn't follow it at all. I just know the key words were "Russia," "Ukraine," and "Crimea." I remember employees at my client's office watching TV and believing analysts who said this was going to start World War III.

"Buy gold!" they told their investors.

Three months after that, a consumer would have to struggle to find Ukraine or Crimea anywhere in the papers. Gold dipped lower and lower. That story became old news... just like the swine flu scare of 2009 and Ebola scare of 2014... and coming hyperinflation in 2009, 2010, 2011, 2012, all the way up to infinity. People in the U.S. had a greater chance of getting heart attacks in their bathtubs while showering than getting Ebola or swine flu.

There will not be another World War during our lifetimes... not if the United Nations is around. The worst-case scenario would be the World vs. North

Korea or the World vs. Islamist nations... but not another World War.

4) High-level executives run the media. They have the power to control stories.

Left-wing governments, corporate spin doctors and lobbyists can control the liberal news media. By the same token, right-wing governments, corporate spin doctors and lobbyists can control the conservative news media. They all create their own stories or spin current ones in their favor. They leak whatever images or video they choose to rile up the public. They tell spokespeople exactly what to say.

For example, a friend of mine was in Ukraine during the worst of the Crimea conflict. I asked him how scary it was, and he said watching the news report on the conflict was news to him. He said he thought all the bad stuff was happening in areas that he never visited a few miles away from him. He didn't see any of the harsh footage we were fed here in the U.S. In fact, he said there are some parts of every major city in the U.S. that are worse than what Ukraine looked like.

There are professional public relations firms that specialize in "innovative events." They pay actors and actresses to protest their clients' causes.

Take a look at a Craigslist job description from this well-known Los Angeles-based (near Hollywood, of course) firm, Crowds on Demand:

> *"Our events include everything from rallies to protests to corporate PR stunts to celebrity scenes. The biggest qualification is enthusiasm, a "can-do" spirit. Pay will vary by event but typically is $25+ per hour plus reimbursements for gas/parking/Uber/public transit."*

This is how Crowds on Demand describes itself:

> *"Your home for Protests, Rallies, Audiences, PR Stunts, and Celebrity Events. Are you looking to create a buzz anywhere in the United States? At Crowds on Demand, we provide our clients with protests, rallies, flash-mobs, paparazzi events and other inventive PR stunts. These services are available across the country in every major U.S city, every major U.S metro area and even most smaller cities as well. We provide everything including the people, the materials and even the ideas. We've made campaigns involving hundreds of people come to action in just days. We have a proven record of delivering major*

wins on even the toughest campaigns and delivering phenomenal experiences with even the most logistically challenging events."

When you watch TV or listen to the news, you're being fed the worst, most outlandish footage, sound bites, and sources. It's not real, so don't believe it.

Another example: during the George Zimmerman / Trayvon Martin days, the media used the term "white Hispanic" to describe Zimmerman, a neighborhood watchman who shot – in self-defense – the African-American Trayvon Martin dead. The term "white Hispanic" fit the narrative, and it packed a bigger punch than just saying, "Hispanic kills black teen."

For months, the media and politicians referred to Trump loyalists as "uneducated whites" or "non-college-educated whites." You know what the media and politicians called this same group when they voted in HUGE numbers for Obama in 2008 and 2012? "Rural America." Same person, different label based solely on who they voted for.

Rural voters in Pennsylvania, Ohio, Wisconsin, and Iowa who voted for Obama in 2008 but Trump in

2016... did the mainstream news media label them as racist back then too? Or just this time around?

For decades, the former CEO of FOX News Roger Ailes (rest in peace) publicly stated that he was "in the ratings business." He never said he was in the journalism business or the truth-telling business.

A producer for a major news outlet once told me that his job "was to fill the space in between ads." He said he told reporters to embellish stories or facts about the economy.

The mainstream media does this all the time. Their shows are "cast" just like dramas to make them more appealing TO GET RATINGS. That's what it's all about.

Our college news outlets at Syracuse did a far better job of covering stories than for-profit media enterprises.

Again, don't believe the media. Don't believe the words you read or hear.

I don't actively watch or read the news. I prefer not to be misinformed.

The next bullet explains in further detail...

5) Mainstream news is inaccurate.

Bullet 4 previously tells you the news media's hidden agendas...

People are better off without the spin of the press. Time after time, there has been misinformation from the mainstream, which leads to misinformed Facebook posts and emotions.

For example, I pulled up Trump's 2017 Executive Order to ban certain immigrants from seven predominantly Muslim countries and read it from beginning to end. I compared it to what the *New York Times* and CNN reported on it. I then went back to read Obama's *Terrorist Travel Prevention Act of 2015* and compared it to the Executive Order.

The results were staggering: none of the mainstream covered the Executive Order properly. People on social media were pent up without knowing the details. It's like what the media covered and what the actual Executive Order said were two different documents and storylines.

Another example of the media creating misinformation: there was an email from an immigration attorney being passed around the Indian community after Trump's immigration ban. The attorney asked Indians to cancel all their flights anywhere and to stay at home for the entire 2017 year because the Executive Order was targeting all browns and more bad news would be coming for Indians. She said to call her law office first before doing any travel or leaving the home.

Several Indians sent this to me on WhatsApp. I called the lawyer directly, and I discovered that she was just trying to scam fellow Indians (as I expected). She was no different from the mainstream media. She had bills to pay in New York City and was doing what she could to get by – even if it meant misleading or scaring people.

Example 3: Despite being associated with all sorts of political parties throughout his career, Trump was a lifelong supporter of Democrats and liberal policies until a few years before the 2012 Election (likely because he was plotting to run as a Republican in 2015). He ran for President in 2000 as a Reformer who wanted universal healthcare, Oprah as his VP, and socialist Charlie Rangel in his Cabinet – far from conservative or Republican. Nobody knew Trump was a Republican until he declared his candidacy in 2015. The Republican Party still does not consider him to be a true Republican.

The average brainwashed, news consuming citizen has no clue about any of this...

Brainwashed people don't know they're brainwashed. If they knew, then they wouldn't be brainwashed.

If you are doing well or reaching your goals, news will spread lies about you...

But it's important to show pity for such liars...

It's very likely that lying is all they have going for themselves. Without the lies, the mainstream news media would continue to struggle financially.

All mainstream media outlets are owned by one entity, and that's FNN: The Fake News Network.

So, if you're concerned about all the fake news, the solution is simple: go directly to the primary sources.

6) **The media uses scare tactics.**

So many news stories have scared my friends and family. They bought investment x, y, z and regretted it. They took money out of the markets and regretted it. They moved their families and regretted it.

One friend of mine read a news article that said the stock market was going to decline 50% within a year. This was in 2009. That friend got scared and took all his money out.

What was the source? Who knows.

Who was the writer? Who cares!

That friend (who has a PhD but obviously not in finance) has been saying the market will go down 50% ever since... all because of that stupid blog post he read a decade ago!

Right-wing conservatives (FOX News: you should be ashamed) said Obama would destroy America. Obama is out of office, and the U.S is in a better position now than before he was in office.

They also said Obama would destroy our lives. I can tell you my life hasn't changed at all from 2008 (when Obama was elected) to now because of anything Obama did. No politician has controlled my decisions to attend school, move places, date women, start businesses, or even pay taxes! You want to find ways to legally pay fewer taxes? Then hire a good accountant. It's that simple.

Want to actually be fearful or see destruction? Go to some of these countries in Eastern Europe, South America (Venezuela right now), or any war-torn country in the Middle East or Africa.

I've gotten older and more mature since 2008. I've done some cool things. I've been depressed. I've been heartbroken.

Thank you, Obama, for having nothing to do with any of this!

Bottom line: no politician or news report changed my life's progression. The times I've listened to them, I've found myself regretting it.

People will believe anything, and the media knows that. The term "fear" in the US is a joke to get people scared. There are entire industries that prey on naive and misinformed individuals so those individuals can take out their credit cards to buy something... products, advertising, time. It's all a scam to hit your emotions.

Democracy is the process of appealing to the unsophisticated masses who can't distinguish between entertainment and politics. Donald Trump is a show businessman, and politics is show business for ugly people... thanks to the mainstream news media.

7) The media is a business too. It needs to make money to survive.

News outlets embellish or make up fake stories for ratings. It's been going on for centuries. These are businesses, and it's all about ratings for them. That's how they make their money.

Prior to the Election of 2016, news media subscription revenue was way down across the board. Advertising was too.

There's too much free content online. The only way news organizations can survive is by sensationalizing or offering information that is so specialized that people would pay a premium for it.

Forget about reporters or journalists making mistakes. Mistakes happen and are forgivable.

CNN has already publicly reprimanded or fired tens of reporters post-Trump Election. Are the reporters at fault?

No, the fake news and intentional negligence starts at the top.

Project Veritas exposed CNN producer John Bonifield in an undercover sting:

"[Russia] is ratings. Our [CNN] ratings are incredible right now.

"[The whole Russia thing] is mostly bullshit right now. We don't have any giant proof. Then, they [CNN] say, 'Well, there's still an investigation going on.' The President is probably right to say, like, 'Look, you are witch-hunting me. You have no smoking gun, you have no real proof.'

"All the nice cutesy little ethics that used to get talked about in journalism school are just like, 'That's adorable.' This is a business, especially cable news. Cable news isn't the *New York Times*. It's not even NBC News. NBC News still gets 20 million viewers a night. Cable news is getting a million. They gotta do what they gotta do to make their money."

***

A few weeks after being elected, Donald Trump held a sit-down "media summit" at the Trump Tower in New York City. All the major mainstream media networks sent top spokespeople: Jeff Zucker, Chuck Todd, Lester Holt, Charlie Rose, George Stephanopoulos, Erin Burnett were among those in attendance. The *New York*

Post reported it wasn't a summit, rather a "firing squad" where Trump criticized reporters, anchors, and their employers.

You know what? It's about damn time somebody – particularly a politician – had the balls to get all the charlatans in one room and not be afraid to call them the frauds they are, one by one...

Reading books and newsletters related to your hobbies and interests are great. Listening to podcasts are real...

But reading or watching the news is a scam and a complete waste of attention.

People shouldn't be putting their faith in the media. That is a disastrous prescription.

People should instead be putting more faith in themselves. It's our job to succeed regardless of what CNN or the *New York Times* is reporting.

Some people are so lazy and myopic that they must have their minds controlled, be fed corporate propaganda, and have information hidden from them. For example, a radio producer told me that a station told him that he COULD NOT mention Bernie Sanders on the air.

Unfortunately, there are people who feel so threatened by freedom of thought and information that they would rather be lied to, manipulated, managed like sheep and told what to do.

Don't become a victim.

Best of luck.

Chapter 4

HOW DONALD TRUMP NEWSJACKED HIS WAY TO FREE PUBLICITY

This book is about digital liberals helping Donald Trump get elected. Digital liberals didn't even know it, and they still refuse to accept it.

People who follow politics become so brainwashed because of the information they're consuming. Brainwashed people don't know they're brainwashed. If they knew, then they wouldn't be brainwashed.

The left-wing liberal news media is just as responsible for Trump becoming President than left-wing digital liberals... and the mainstream media knows it...

There were entire industries with businesses models dependent on Barack Obama being President, just so they could hate on him to generate traffic. The same applies to Trump...

CNN President Jeff Zucker told the Hollywood Reporter that 2016 was CNN's best year ever for ratings thanks to Donald Trump. Their primetime viewership was up 50 percent, and showings among adults 25-54 were up 55 percent. The Deadline also reported that

CNN, FOX and MSNBC scored the largest Presidential Debate ratings in their histories.

New York Times subscriptions have also soared 11-fold... all because of Trump.

From the start, Trump made politically incorrect statements that surprised the public. He mastered the art of *newsjacking* – the science of injecting one's ideas into a breaking news story so the ideas and their creator get noticed.

Trump took major world events and added his own doom and gloom hyperbole to sell his ideas – and himself. The basic formula for newsjacking:

For example, after a major Islamic terrorist attack at a gay nightclub in Orlando, tensions were extremely high among people from all political and religious ideologies. The event dominated news headlines and social media for weeks.

In response, Trump called for a ban on Muslims entering the United States. Never mind that banning anyone and everyone from a religion is unconstitutional... it was a bold proposal, but one that generated a lot of interest from fringe voters who were legitimately afraid for their safety.

It's one thing to acknowledge a news event like all the other politicians did: "We will fight terrorism!" or "My thoughts and prayers go out to the victims."

It's another thing to immediately offer solutions on the spot – no matter how dumb they may be.

The entire 2016 Election was about Trump. The media had to cover something, so they gave Trump free coverage, PR and advertising, which allowed him to spend less than half of what Hillary Clinton spent on her campaign, as reported by CNBC.

In fact, Trump was so good at "newsjacking" that Hillary Clinton ran ads about him. She featured him in her commercials – not herself. She was spending millions of dollars to tell the public not to vote for Trump and giving Trump more airtime instead of promoting herself and telling people to vote for her.

Hillary Clinton commented, "When they [Trump camp] go low, we go high." Instead, she might as well as have said, "When they go low, we go low too."

Hillary had an "us vs. him" message. Trump had an "us vs. them" message. That is a major reason why he won, and Hillary lost.

This book has touched on how Trump believes strongly in building and owning businesses. He won the Election while spending far less than Hillary, who also had two Presidents, the First Lady, Beyoncé, Jay-Z, Lebron James, Bruce Springsteen, a string of media surrogates, every rapper on earth, an army of circus clowns, four Greek gods, and a cheerleading squad backing her push to the White House.

Trump may be an assh*le and very offensive, but you can't say he wasn't efficient.

Trump spoke the language to the middle-class layman. The way he talked... he convinced them he's not a billionaire. He's just like them... and because he's one of them, people stopped looking at the problems and put their faith "In Donald We Trust."

In the end, all the negative publicity helped Trump more than it hurt him. The saying goes, "There is no such thing as bad publicity." The next chapter explains why in greater detail.

Chapter 5

HOW DIGITAL LIBERALS ELECTED PRESIDENT DONALD TRUMP

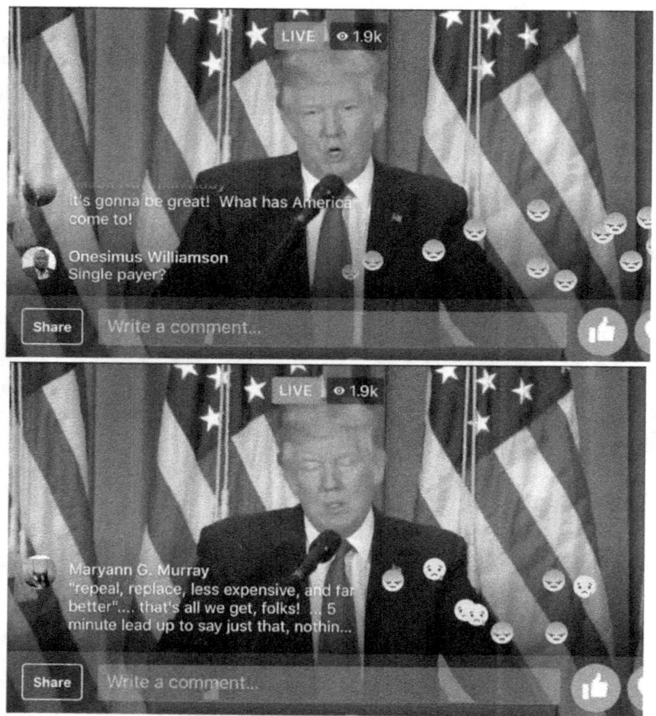

Artificial intelligence entrepreneur Sanjiv Rai developed a machine to predict political winners based on online and digital media "engagements." The system is 100% accurate in US and global elections. It predicted Donald Trump winning the GOP when he wasn't even a top five candidate in polls and predicted Trump defeating Hillary because his "digital engagements" were higher than Obama's in 2008 and 2012.

During the GOP primaries, there were immense amounts of negative coverage about Trump, and despite this, he creamed his competition by receiving the most GOP primary votes EVER.

It's Newton's Third Law applied to the electoral process: equal but opposite. For as many haters there are, there are an equal number of lovers.

In Trump's case, he's already won the social media engagement accolade of being the most hated President ever... and that's exactly why he was elected President in the first place. It's why Obama won in 2012 amid Benghazi, the Birther Movement and Obamacare debacles, and it's why George W. Bush won in 2004 during a worthless debacle of wars in the Middle East and Afghanistan.

The strategy is called divide and conquer. It's nothing new. Alexander the Great did it. Genghis Khan did it. Fidel Castro, FDR, Winston Churchill, George

Washington all did it. Aurangzeb did it during the Moghul dynasty, and Narendra Modi is doing it in India now. It's why Adolph Hitler had a shot at taking over the world. He was the closest to doing so post-status quo antebellum. It's the oldest Machiavellian strategy to gain control and power.

The US has been a divided nation since Thomas Jefferson and the advent of bipartisanship.

Where was all the shit talk about Romney and McCain in 2012 and 2008? It was weak... nothing compared to Trump.

And guess what? Romney and McCain both lost in landslides. They weren't hated enough by the Left to win. They were boring candidates.

If you don't want to divide people, then don't run for political office. You won't win.

The digital liberals can't get enough of Trump. They are the reason he's been so relevant. They watch all his press conferences and whine on Facebook and Twitter during and after. They read any news article about him — even if it is fake. They seriously pray — even if they're atheist — that he will be impeached. There is proof after proof of their obsession with him.

Complaining about Donald Trump on social media feels good to digital liberals, but it doesn't create any solutions or accomplish anything.

This does not mean the candidate who's shit on the most will win. It merely means the candidate who's talked about the most will win. It's the talk that guys like Romney, McCain, Rand Paul, Mike Huckabee, and John Kerry would've killed for.

In other words, if nobody is talking about you, you have no chance at winning.

Masses of digital liberals and mainstream media propelled Trump to get to where he is today. Three years before the Election, he wasn't a top 500 candidate. Two years before, he wasn't in the top 100.

Donald Trump was not elected by his voters. It was his biggest detractors – mainstream liberal news media, loudmouth liberals, and digital liberals alike – who built up his support and kept his campaign running.

The digital liberals still don't understand that by relentlessly attacking Trump, they're actually helping him. Had all of them spent more energy hating on Dr. Ben Carson or Dr. Rand Paul, or if they just didn't bother talking about Trump, then Hillary Clinton would've punched her ticket to the White House.

You don't beat Trump by giving him more attention. You beat him by making him irrelevant. Do not love or hate him. Ignore him.

2016 was the most followed election of our lifetimes because of Trump. Hillary ran in 2008, and people didn't give a crap. She got smoked by a nobody (Barack Obama) who ended up bringing change to public discourse and the political process... for better or for worse. Trump is doing the same – bringing about change to public discourse and the political process... for better or for worse.

The mainstream polls, like Quinnipiac University National, showed that Hillary had it in the bag the summer before the Election of 2016. She was the talk of the GOP debates. The mainstream polls also showed she had an insurmountable lead after the Democratic National Convention (DNC) despite her low approval ratings and again after Trump's comments about p*ssies.

Things only got close because of the attention people and the media gave Trump. He brought fear and hullabaloo to every debate, yet his numbers in Florida, Ohio and North Carolina rose thanks to the moderators' questions being centered around his controversies over Hillary's, every media outlet covering his poor performance rather than Hillary's strong showings, and millions of people posting negative things about him instead of positive things about Hillary.

Digital liberals are responsible for Trump winning because they decided that other opinions and ways of looking at the world are unacceptable. If you call a digital liberal out on his or her baseless opinion or don't agree with them, then you're labeled a freak, evil, stupid idiot, racist, xenophobe, or deplorable.

How do you think people are going to vote if you talk to them like that?

The more digital liberals whine, cry and insult, the more the "Silent 49%" will grow. The Silent 49% was so shamed that they let their votes do the talking.

Chapter 6

WHY MOST OF THE CABINET IS WORTHLESS

Facebook Posts:

"I cried after I heard Trump named Betsy DeVos as Education Secretary. our public schools will be close. Their will b no more educate people. Kids have no future."

*"Ben Carson ain't no Docter. That ni*ga Dr. Tom."*

"Mnuchin is a Goldman bureaucrat who killed our economy ten years ago. Goldman guys kill U.S. economies. It's been proven throughout history. Mnuchin has no place in financial or economic policy."

The aforementioned Betsy DeVos poster is confused, and it's truly sad it was written by a public elementary school teacher. She has no idea that she's borderline illiterate, yet she is "crying" because she thinks DeVos will tarnish "America's stellar, superb, world-leading public school system," said no person ever. I highly doubt the poster had ever heard of "Betsy DeVos" until the media went off on her rich, aristocratic background and her ideas on school choice and the privatization of schools.

The Secretary of Education – just like the Secretary of Energy and Secretary of Housing & Urban Development (HUD) – doesn't do jack sh*t. Most educated and "informed" people can't even name two former Secretaries of Education, and they don't understand how little federal government plays in education compared to the states. The nightmares this poster is having about all public schools shutting down and kids having nowhere to go to learn is completely unjustified.

If people think the Secretary of Education is so powerful, then look at the previous education secretaries who have contributed to the destruction of public education: rising dropout rates, stagnant literacy rates, rising murder rates, declining homeownership rates. A case can be made that their policies have led to extreme decay, joblessness, and total chaos.

A report funded by the Bill and Melinda Gates Foundation calls high school dropout rates a "national catastrophe." NBC News reports that every school day, nearly 7,000 children drop out of school. If you do the math, that means more than a million students drop out every year.

Education should not be about politics. The person leading it should have a human decency to do what is necessary to provide adequate educational opportunities for Americans – not someone who has no compassion for those whom he/she is supposed to be serving.

Never value politics over education. The latter elevates you. The former allows others to exploit you for their own financial gain.

Betsy DeVos has devoted her late life to education reform and policy. She looks at education in a way that is not consistent with the norm of administration, teaching, or public bureaucracy.

"The world's dumbest and poorest are educated by private schools." Even most illiterates know this isn't true.

Competition drives value and efficiency. A lack of competition drives absolutely nothing. Markets only work well when they are subject to competition. Services improve when people are free to "shop around" and when competitive pressures inspire suppliers (educators) to invent better ways of doing things.

People who believe in school choice know they are not the property of the Democratic or Republican parties. I personally wouldn't leave my child in a failing school while waiting 40 years for a political party to finally fix the education system.

Inside Higher Ed reports that the average child spends roughly 14,000 hours in school before he or she graduates high school, yet nearly 20% of the graduates are near illiterate. Why are so many kids who graduate from public school still not able to read?

If you want to be a truly powerless person, just keep blindly putting faith into the country's education systems.

DeVos recognizes that the destruction of the family is the root cause of many educational and formative issues...

Single parent households aren't bad, but the data is not favorable for the future of their children...

The *Single Mother Guide* found that unwed mothers are four times more likely to live in poverty than the average American. Female-headed families earn only 40% as much as two-parent families. Not only do unmarried mothers tend to earn relatively little, but their households are limited to a single breadwinner – thus further widening the income gap between one-parent and two-parent families. 85% of all children in poverty live in single-parent, mother-child homes.

Two-parent families are rarely poor. Among families where both the husband and wife work full-time, the current poverty rate is a mere 2%.

Children in single-parent households are also raised with social and psychological disadvantages. For instance, they are four times as likely as children from intact families to be abused or neglected; much likelier to have trouble academically; twice as prone to drop out of school; three times more likely to have behavioral problems; two-and-a-half times likelier to be sexually active as teens; twice as likely to conceive children out-of-wedlock when they are teens or young adults; and three times likelier to be on welfare when they reach adulthood.

How can an Education Secretary fix parenting so that kids grow up in two-parent households?

In addition, Pew Research Center found that 70% of all young people in state reform institutions were raised in fatherless homes, as were 60% of rapists, 72% of adolescent murderers, and 70% of long-term prison inmates.

Illegitimacy is a major factor in America's education problem. Lack of two parents (whether separated but involved, or together as one) could be the principal factor in high school graduation rates and academic competency.

I have no clue what's right or wrong. My opinion doesn't matter.

But I do know that it is important to keep an open mind to all thoughts, even if they are unconventional. It doesn't matter who proposes solutions or what political party they're affiliated with.

These are very complicated issues, which is why I'm open to new ideas... because what's been done so far hasn't been working well.

Regardless, much of whatever bad – or good – DeVos can do as the Secretary of Education will be undone by a future Administration holding a different view. That's how it's always worked.

As a fiscal conservative and free market enthusiast, I think the greatest thing that can come from DeVos: she turns out to be so dumb and clueless that the Democrats try to abolish her position and the Department of Education.

***

A similar justification can be made for Dr. Ben Carson as the Secretary of Housing & Urban Development (HUD)...

The previous HUDs have contributed to the destruction of inner cities. *FiveThirtyEight* cites rising murder rates and the *Wall Street Journal* cites declining homeownership rates. A case can be made that the policies of previous HUDs have only led to extreme urban decay, joblessness, and total chaos.

HUD should not be about politics. The person leading it should have a human decency of doing what is necessary to provide adequate housing opportunities for the American taxpayers — not someone who has no compassion for those whom he/she is supposed to be serving.

Dr. Carson is very intelligent and cares about the urban community. He's not a Clarence Thomas. He looks at the urban community in a way that is not consistent with the norm. He is right about the destruction of the family as the root cause of many inner-city problems.

Dr. Carson is the first HUD Secretary to be born and raised in an urban area AND *qualify* for public housing. Dr. Carson said in a speech at Yale University that his mother chose not to live in public housing because she wanted to keep her kids away from danger and violence.

It is important for people to keep their minds open to any and all ideas that might work, even if they are unconventional. It doesn't matter who proposes solutions or what political party they're affiliated with.

These are very complicated issues, which is why I'm open to new ideas... because what's been done so far hasn't been working well.

As a fiscal conservative and free market enthusiast, I think the greatest thing that can come from Dr. Carson:

he turns out to be so clueless that the Democrats try to abolish his position and the Department of Housing & Urban Development.

***

Steve Mnuchin is thankfully not in the same categories as previous Goldman Sachs Treasury Secretaries. Unlike other Goldman corporatists, Mnuchin went out on his own – using his own capital – to form private equity firms and hedge funds that have created value in various industries, including Hollywood. Some of his most famous titles as Executive Producer include *Avatar, American Sniper, The Devil Wears Prada, X-Men, The Lego Movie, Mad Max, Batman v Superman, Keanu, The Legend of Tarzan, Sully,* and *Suicide Squad.*

Mnuchin's not your bureaucratic banker – and he's not partisan either. His success on Wall Street and Hollywood led him to donate lots of money to the Clintons and other Democrats. He worked for and supported left-wing nut George Soros but also lived and worked with Eddie Lambert, an Ayn Rand libertarian fiend who was touted as a rising Warren Buffett in his 30s.

Mnuchin has a far better idea about how jobs are created in middle America and how books are balanced.

In any case, the Federal Reserve, which controls interest rates, has way more influence on monetary policy and the future of the markets and global economy than any Treasury Secretary.

Chapter 7

WHY DO KANYE WEST AND OTHER AFRICAN-AMERICANS SUPPORT DONALD TRUMP?

Facebook Post:

"Kanye West sure likes throwing black folks under the bus. Kanye is racist and wants to further disenfranchise black people and marginalize their grievances. So thank you Kanye West for continuing to ignore the bigger picture, feeding into the white supremacist agenda, and contributing to many more years of public scrutiny towards people of color. I hope you're comfortable licking the boots of a demagogue whose rhetoric has fueled entitled racism to come out of the the cave where it belonged. No matter how good you think a candidate is, you should always draw the line at divisive and racist language. Fuck rap, get your kids to learn something that helps the world so black folks no longer are forced to have men like this represent our opinions. I hope you and all your self hating cronies read this, but it will probably never reach outside this page. In closing you, fuck you you disappointment, we deserve better. #kanyewest #fuckyou #fuckyouKanye #Fuckyoukim"

Wish granted...

I'm glad this poster is getting the therapy he/she sorely needs completely free of charge... through Facebook. I have found writing to be the best therapy – better than over-the-counter pills, prescription meds, yoga, meditation and exercise.

This poster's frustration stemmed from Kanye West telling his Saint Pablo Tour concertgoers a week or two after the Election that he would've voted for Donald Trump had he voted. Right after he said that to a chorus of boos, he busted out his song "Heartless," which the audience started rapping along with him. When Kanye saw this, he cut the song.

"I just said that I would have voted for Donald Trump, and then I did a song and y'all sang it at the top of your lungs," he said. "That doesn't mean that you're a Trump supporter. That just means you OK with a celebrity having their own opinion. Or that someone else is OK to have their own opinion. That might not be your opinion but you can still like that person or still like that person's music."

The people in the audience were confused. Kanye exposed their hypocrisy.

His fans are the same people who voted for Barack Obama in 2008 and 2012 and failed to hit the polls in 2016.

If half the 2016 black non-voters who voted for Obama in 2008 or 2012 had voted for Hillary Clinton, then she'd be President today.

Black voters are not overwhelmingly Trump supporters. The Pew Research Center found that nearly 9% of them voted for him. That's 1 out of 11 people... but if you add up the number of African-Americans who didn't vote at all, which essentially is a vote against Hillary, then you'll see that Trump did quite well in not pissing off African-Americans completely. To put the numbers into further context: the African-American vote for Donald Trump was nearly double Mitt Romney's vote in 2012, according to Pew.

How did President Trump build his African-American support? Unlike previous Republicans and Democrats, Trump addressed blacks personally. He showed up to and donated $30,000 worth of supplies to a Baton Rouge hurricane disaster relief and participated in black church sessions, despite their hostility towards him.

He knew he wouldn't win the black vote, but he said during a black rally in Michigan, "What do you have to lose? You're living in poverty, your schools are no good, you have no jobs, 58% of your youth is unemployed, what the hell do you have to lose?" In other words, he used the following logic on black voters: "You guys don't like or support me right now because you're not happy. Why are you not happy? Why have you been so unhappy for decades? What have Obama, Bill and Hillary Clinton done to improve your lives? You have nothing more to lose by voting for me! Give me a chance!!!"

The media turned Trump into a racist, yet he was rolling with black people throughout his campaign. He even had a staff member – Omarosa Manigault – whose sole job was to connect with the African-American community. Hillary didn't have that... and neither did President Obama.

Senator Hillary Clinton and her husband Bill Clinton (as Governor of Arkansas and President of the United States) got racist laws passed, and citizens didn't find out how racist they were against blacks until years after the damage was done...

The *Daily Beast* reported that the Clintons have incarcerated more blacks than any other family this country has witnessed. There's only been two of them who've been around for four decades post-Civil Rights. The Kennedys, on the other hand, have been around far longer with a lot more people pre-Civil Rights... and the Clintons have still persecuted more blacks.

"I signed a bill that made the problem worse," Hillary Clinton said about black incarceration in July 2016.

Bill and Hillary have been true masters of deception. They can say whatever they want, but that's a horrible history of race relations based on what they've done.

At least we know what we're getting up front with Trump...

A month after Trump won, he had meetings with countless prominent African-Americans, before he even took office: Kanye, Ray Lewis, Steve Harvey, Martin Luther King III are just a fraction of the names. Compare this to eight years of President Obama, who took a vacation during the Million Man March and contributed to the rise of black unemployment, college dropout, homicide and incarceration rates while he was in office.

Newsmax reports that by nearly every economic indicator, blacks were worse off at the end of President Obama's Presidency than when he was sworn into office. During Obama's terms, black Americans experienced record lows in small business loans and saw their lowest homeownership rates in 25 years. This is along with having record highs in unemployment and experiencing large amounts of wealth loss. Since Obama took office, the racial wealth gap grew by more than 30%.

Obama was a great President for gays and white people... but the data shows he did little to help the African-American community in a significant way. If Obama had done half as much for blacks as he did for gays, there would be reparations right now.

It makes no sense to allow shootings and murders in black inner cities to keep rising while still making sure the "lily-white" suburbs stay safe. The digital liberals would call that "racist." Trump has publicly Tweeted he wants to make streets safer for innocent black folk. If he tries doing that, he'd be doing more for the black community than any other President since the 1960's.

In February 2017, President Trump signed a measure to boost government support for the nation's historically black colleges (HBCUs). Trump's order moved the federal government's program for promoting HBCUs back under direct oversight of the White House.

If we're going to be honest about the failings of one President, we must also be honest about the failings of the other...

HBCUs took huge steps backward under President Obama. *The Hill* reports that HBCU enrollment dropped significantly, and more than $170 million in funding was tossed down the drain.

It's rather tragic that President Trump has already done more for historically black colleges and universities (HBCUs) than President Obama did. This is the fault of the Obama Administration for setting the standard so low in the first place.

Kanye's fans complain about a man they didn't vote for, yet they remain silent about a man they put into office?

Trump doesn't have to do much more to significantly outperform Obama in African-American areas. The black unemployment crisis will NEVER be solved by any politician. It will be solved by black entrepreneurs. Entrepreneurship is how all unemployment crises have been solved. If Trump were to simply increase small business lending to urban neighborhoods, which he said he'd do, that would make a huge difference right away. Blacks already build wealth for White, Asian, Arab, and Jewish store owners and entrepreneurs every day. It's time to start helping one another – brother to brother.

Democrats own a monopoly of control in major American inner cities – all the "killing fields" like Chicago, Detroit, Baltimore, New Orleans and St. Louis. Democrats own these inner cities and have owned them for decades. Deep blue states run by liberal Democrats are going broke all over the United States. You can add Connecticut and socialist California to that list, per *Forbes* and *The Mercury News*. Democrats and progressives are largely responsible for much of what is wrong with the inner cities and many oppressions black people and other minorities suffer. Until now, lame Republicans have been too polite to notice this, but Trump has already made building up Black America a priority, calling for a "New Deal for Black America."

The Democrats continue to make the black community easy prey because they know they'll get most their votes without doing anything to help. It's easy for Democrats to get complacent. But when looking at individual swing states, every vote counts... and in this past Election of 2016, the Democrats paid heavy prices, particularly in Ohio, Florida, Pennsylvania, North Carolina, Michigan, and Wisconsin. Polling pundits expected 2-5% of African-Americans – or about 1 out of 20-50 blacks – to vote for Trump... but as previously mentioned, nearly 9% of African-Americans voted for Trump – 1 out of 11 blacks. Had the numbers panned out like experts predicted, then Trump would not have won the close swing states of Florida, Pennsylvania, North Carolina, Michigan and Wisconsin.

Many of the people yelling and screaming about what Trump isn't doing for black people should have been doing so during Obama's presidency. Do-nothing politicians continue to scam citizens. Wait, scratch that... they do nothing for black people, but do lots of things for the rest of America. Most politicians – while they will ignore reparations – also pay little attention to urban violence, allow black unemployment to fester, and do nothing to save horrible schools.

"I can't wait to see how great life is for blacks once Democrats are back in the White House and Congress. Their lives just keep getting better and better every time they're elected," said no intelligent, rational and informed person ever.

Pew Research found Trump got more votes from people of color than any other Republican candidate in history. Mitt Romney and John McCain lacked minority support and would have gone as far as buying such fandom with their riches. It's why Romney ate his words against Trump after the Election and respected the successful campaign he ran.

Kanye's fans are the same people who are at the club on Friday night dancing and rapping to music that talks about burning *ussies on fire and *ussy resting in peace after it's destroyed. How do I know this? Because I go to these clubs on Friday and Saturday nights. I saw a couple of the groupies at Kanye's Saint Pablo concert when he performed in Tampa.

Black boys are being inundated at young ages by violent music. This is because sellout black men make music that hypnotizes young black males to become homicidal drug addicts.

Read these lyrics to the song "Gunwalk" by Lil Wayne. I could easily find hundreds more songs just like this one:

Uh, fuck that ni**a, ho ass ni**a

Leave that ni**a with a toe tag ni**a
Barrel so long, you can pole dance, ni**a
Run up in ya house, where the dope at
ni**a

Murder she wrote on a notepad ni**a
Light that ni**a up, smoke that ni**a
Stomp that ni**a, roast that ni**a
I walk around with this shotgun
And this b*tch bigger than me ni**a
Don't open up yo fuckin' mouth
Cause I'll pull the trigger like teeth ni**a
Shoot 'em up, then leave ni**a
I smell summer's eve ni**a
We shoot first, it's better
To give than receive ni**a

Anyone with any understanding of the subconscious mind would never think it's good for millions of black kids to listen to music that teaches them to murder or abuse one another. Rappers who spit out hateful, poisonous and genocidal lyrics pose an imminent threat to the survival of children. Want to have a horrible life? All you need to do is drink heavily and use drugs — particularly at an early age.

If the average rapper represents your future, then you'll end up in a prison cell or dead.
If Donald Trump represents your future, well then, at least you can plan to become a billionaire and President of the United States.

Rappers who promote drug addiction to masses of people on the radio and the Internet are far worse than Donald Trump being President. I would even say these Black KKK members are worse than the real KKK, who affects less than 1% of the U.S. population... but such a statement would get me into trouble with the digital liberals, so I won't say that.

DrugFree.org reports that drug use has been rising in this country – not declining – and approximately 24 million Americans are addicted to alcohol and drugs. To put that number into context: one in every 10 Americans over the age of 12 – roughly equal to the entire population of Texas – are smoking or sipping on syrup, bud, purple drank, weed, molly, blow, Percocet, or sticky icky.

Kanye knows his fans better than anyone else. They'd much rather pay to attend his concerts than vote for President, and then they moan and boo for no reason outside of, "Trump is racist." Their defense for anything and everything is, "That's racist."

Most of them have no clue how to negotiate better trade deals, how to fight terrorists, how wealth is created, the pros and cons of tax cuts, or the threat open borders pose to their lifestyles and safety. Instead, they spew hate, refuse to mingle with people different from themselves, and whine about "racism."

I'm astonished that it took a Donald Trump for so many digital liberals to recently realize that racism exists. Maybe I've just seen it more growing up in Texas and attending a 96% white high school.

It's hard to get a grasp of people in this country when you live in socialist republics like New York, Maryland and California [where a bulk of the digital liberals referenced in this book reside(d)].

"Things won't change until people admit their own falsehoods," Kanye said at his concert after ticking off his fans. "Specifically to black people, stop focusing on racism. This world is racist, OK? Let's stop being distracted to focus on that as much. It's just a f**king fact. We are in a racist country. Period... not one or the other candidate was going to instantly change that."

Fellow rapper Snoop Dogg responded, "I smoke weed. What the fuck is Kanye on?"

Kanye's on truth, Snoop.

How is someone so correct so consistently derided?

Because people can't handle the truth...

Kanye and Kim are smarter, more knowledgeable and connected than people give them credit for.

#Kanye2024 #KimFirstLady

Chapter 8

WHY PRESIDENTS HAVE NOTHING TO DO WITH POLICE BRUTALITIES

Facebook Post:

"This woman is stopped and questioned because of the color of her skin while walking in her home neighborhood, because she looked suspicious. When was the last time a cop stopped you because you looked different? Folks, wake up. This is not about Red and Blue, about Republican and Democrat. If at all you are a honest 'decent' person and who judges someone by who he is and not because of what he looks like — you need to start showing your dissent of the President and his abhorrent racist actions. Trump is brainwashing cops to be racist. He is turning the country into a racist state."

This Facebook poster is referring to an incident that happened with Aravinda Pillalamarri, an Indian American activist who's been instrumental in promoting social justice to poor villages in India. Pillalamarri was walking around her suburban Baltimore neighborhood when she was stopped for questioning by a cop because a neighbor reported her for suspicious activity.

The only problem with this Facebook post is... IT HAS ABSOLUTELY NOTHING TO DO WITH DONALD TRUMP, who wasn't even President when this episode occurred.

Charging someone with racism, bigotry, xenophobia, sexism or any other left-wing extreme word is a huge accusation. Such labels can destroy a name, word, reputation and future. Post-Election 2016, these words are being thrown around in everyday language, and there are no repercussions for using such terms. Being labeled as a racist in this country has become just as bad as worshiping Hitler or raping a child.

If someone reports suspicious activity to the cops, then what are the cops supposed to do? Nothing?

Is the neighbor an idiot for reporting suspicious activity?

People call the cops because they want to feel safer. The neighbors in this story didn't call the cops to be racist. If they wanted to be truly racist, they could've done much worse things. The neighbors called the cops for precautionary purposes.

In the case of the 2015 San Bernardino terrorists, the *Daily Mail* reported that neighbors saw Syed Rizwan Farook and his wife Tashfeen Malik doing shady things and acting suspicious, but they didn't report the couple to the cops because they didn't want to create drama and be known in the neighborhood as racists or ethnic profilers. Farook and Malik ended up executing the biggest husband-wife terrorist attack in U.S. history. These neighbors could've saved 14 lives and another few dozens' mental and physical well beings.

I will even admit... when I was in graduate school at Duke University, I called security because there was a shady looking black man driving around our apartment lot. There were daily thefts and assaults going on in Durham. I would've rather been safe than sorry. It turned out I called security on one of their guards who was patrolling the area in a non-security car 😄.

The poster asks, "When was the last time a cop stopped you because you looked different?"

Where has this person been living the past 20 years? Has he not followed #BlackLivesMatter at all? Or looked up the term "racial profiling"? It's been happening forever... literally. It still happens every day today.

A few weeks after 9/11, my father was detained near the Texas-Mexico border while he was working offshore (he's a structural engineer for deepwater oil rigs). It was early October – peak allergy season for him – and he was wearing an allergy mask.

Brown man + allergy mask = police questioning... that's the equation.

When my father was released from questioning, he didn't whine or complain. In fact, he was thankful the authorities were doing their job to keep the country safe.

People should want to feel safe. Neighbors don't call the cops on their neighbors to be racist. If they call the cops and give this reason, then the cops would laugh at them and carry on with their day. Neighbors call cops because they feel some sort of threat to their safety.

I can promise you that neighbor learned from their mistake and will never call the cops ignorantly on a Hindu woman again.

Blaming Trump for Pillalamarri's questioning is akin to blaming Barack Obama for Sureshbhai Patel's police assault in Alabama or the #BlackLivesMatter assaults and killings. Sureshbhai was stopped while walking around his son's neighborhood in Alabama because a neighbor reported him for suspicious activity... because of his skin color. He was then brutally assaulted by the police because he couldn't speak English.

There are hundreds of other cases like this during every Administration post-Reagan. More reported police brutalities happened under Obama than any other

President, according to *The Nation...* but that's not a reflection of the former President. Obama's Presidency occurred during a time when smartphone cameras hit the mass market, so people could capture such violence and post them publicly.

Let's blame the President for all shortcomings. Every person of color has faced racism in this country. It's not because of the President.

Cops can be idiots. Maryland cops can be bigger idiots. Baltimore cops can be some of the biggest idiots – outright bad or unlawful.

I don't see freedom when fellow Indians are destroyed by fat idiot police officers... or their convenient stores or places of worship are raided for no reasons.

Does that mean I should also blame the country as a whole for such a problem?

The people who carry out such atrocities are idiots. Go after them... not the flag, monument, statue, national anthem or person who wrote the national anthem.

America is not violently racist. President Obama never got a machete and chopped off a citizens' head. He has never murdered or imprisoned anyone who's challenged the government.

At times, the suspects are some fat idiot cops or security. Other times, they're violent murderers who have no respect for human life. That doesn't mean the entire country is like this.

I just got back from a restaurant, and the white waitresses were really nice to me. When I go out tonight, I'll be on the lookout for some racist shit... since that's what digital liberals say this "country is on" and is all pervasive. I'll be sure to take videos and pictures too. It's everywhere.

NOT!

But of course, it's easy to blame one man for all problems...

Facebook Post:

Have had a cold pretty much all of 2017 and then I get food poisoning. Thanks, Trump!

Have diarrhea today? Thanks Trump!

Got a flat tire? Thanks Trump!

Fired from work? Thanks Trump!

I'm no doctor, but maybe if these people stopped thinking about Trump 24/7, they'd feel better.

Chapter 9

WHY PRESIDENTS HAVE NOTHING TO DO WITH RIOTS OR HISTORICAL MONUMENTS

Facebook Post:

"Donald Trump is a disgrace to the people he represents and is an embarrassment to all of us who live in the United States. These Confederate monuments belong in a museum not in the public. Last time I checked we don't celebrate runners up, let alone racists. We must remember history so we do not repeat it but we must not encourage racism by leaving up such monuments. Please join me this weekend in fighting against this atrocity! Adios! It's time to clean house."

If President Donald Trump is a disgrace to the people he represents, then why are his supporters still so enthusiastic about him? As of the publishing of this book in Q4 2017, Rasmussen — one of the most accurate polling sources of the 2016 Election along with The University of Southern California and Investor's Business Daily — has Trump at 52% approval.

Rasmussen also reported that Trump is MORE popular on this date of his presidency than Obama was.

Why does Vegas (Paddy Power, Odds Shark, Odds Checker) project Trump to win the 2020 Election in a landslide fashion? This comes after months of the most biased, vicious, negative media coverage in modern history... where much of the mainstream media tried to destroy, slander, libel, excoriate, impeach, and convict Trump. This same media lied & committed fraud to make Obama a God... yet Trump is still MORE popular.

After firing the FBI Director...

After "obstruction of justice" accusations and investigations...

After nonstop damaging leaks of his conversations with world leaders...

After never-ending accusations of collusion and passing classified information to Russian leaders...

After the media cornering Trump into "supporting" white supremacism...

Donald Trump's party's record (which he has endorsed and is responsible for) is 5-0 in Special Elections since he won in November 2016.

5-0... as in undefeated. Perfect.

What a disgrace!

***

The United States and its Founding Fathers have a history of racism. George Washington owned slaves. Thomas Jefferson raped slaves. Even Abraham Lincoln was not an abolitionist. The History Channel reports that in the fourth Lincoln-Douglas debate well before the Civil War, Lincoln made his position clear:

"I will say then that I am not, nor ever have been, in favor of bringing about in any way the social and political equality of the white and black races," he began, going on to say that he opposed blacks having the right to vote, to serve on juries, to hold office and to intermarry with whites.

We have monuments, statues and holidays dedicated to these former presidents and patriots.

When I think of Bill Clinton, I recollect how he incarcerated more blacks than any other President in history. I also think about how he put a cigar in his intern's tw*t and sucked on it.

Does that mean we remove portraits of U.S. presidents? Is it time to blow up Mount Rushmore? The liberals can go ahead and bulldoze the Washington Monument and Jefferson Memorial in D.C. while they're at it. Already, liberal mainstream media outlet ESPN removed Asian American broadcaster Robert Lee from calling a University of Virginia game in Charlottesville due to his name.

President Trump has absolutely nothing to do with county or municipal statues and monuments. Those are left to the governing bodies that hold jurisdiction.

People don't give a f*ck about tiny little neighborhood monuments. If they did, then the monuments would be controversial topics BEFORE city halls and counties vote on them, not after. People would assemble for riots to pressure politicians or voters ahead of referendums.

A few months before the Election of 2016, the Pew Research Center reported the top 15 issues American voters cared about. Confederate monuments and statues did not make the list. I'll go out on a limb and guess it likely didn't make any top 100 lists either. I tried looking everywhere on the Internet for this issue BEFORE it hit the mainstream press, and I found nothing. Nobody was talking about it before.

I've never thought about statues or monuments a day in my life. If you ask most people, they'll tell you they haven't spent a day of their lives deeply thinking about statues or monuments either.

In Tampa, for example, Hillsborough County commissioners voted to keep a Confederate monument. There was outrage among people after this decision hit the news.

Why weren't people complaining about the statues from the beginning BEFORE voting was conducted?

Because people didn't even know about these statues... they didn't know where they were located. They had never seen them. They still haven't.

In "killing fields" like Detroit, Baltimore and New Orleans, the problem is not white on black crime in the hood. It's black-on-black crime.

Instead of worrying about the damn statue nobody knows or cares about, fix the issues in your own neighborhoods. No sane people have personal problems because of a slave trader named Yale hundreds of years ago.

The taking down of statues is not going to appease the people demanding such measures. After the statues come down, they will demand something else.

The masses who complain on social media and participate in these riots (both liberals and conservatives, black, white, and everything in between) like to worry and complain. They are bored with their lives. They choose not to confront their own deeper personal issues.

They have no clue about history. They are fed lies by government history textbooks, the media, and our politicians.

The status quo ante bellum had slavery ALL over the world on every continent – black-on-black slavery, white-on-black slavery, and even white-on-white slavery. Native Americans took slaves when they conquered another tribe. This is not a white phenomenon but a global one since the dawn of man.

Most people believe European and American slave ships went over and captured free blacks in Africa. This is not true. They sailed over to Tunisian & Libyan ports and purchased from black slave owners.

People in the North and South owned slaves. It wasn't replaced until technology and mechanization came along. It existed for thousands of years prior.

The Civil War was not a war over slavery. The North (Union) did not fight the South (Confederacy) to free the slaves.

The fighting was economic. The South had the right to leave the Union to form its own nation. Those states who are governed can decide how they're governed. This concept still applies today. If Texas or Florida want to start their own countries, they can absolutely secede from the Union to do so. The North had no respect for Southern sovereignty because the South was contributing the extreme majority of GDP, so the North invaded the South. Without the South, the Union would've dissolved economically.

The *Emancipation Proclamation* freeing slaves was signed and delivered by President Lincoln during the thick of the Civil War on January 1, 1863. The Civil War did not end until May 1865. That means the war went on for nearly 2 ½ years even after the slaves were officially freed, no questions asked. Were these armies fighting for no reason?

No, there were many reasons to preserve the Union – chiefly selfish economic motives – none of which had to do with slavery.

Lincoln and the Union were losing the War so badly. He had to emancipate the slaves to hurt the Confederacy economically and tactically so the North could keep the Union intact and have a chance at winning the war.

The United States is the most compassionate, generous, humanitarian, and philanthropic country ever known to man. Our record of services is second to none, and we owe this to our Founding Fathers.

FYI the Nazis removed statues and censored speech they didn't like just before World War II.

The same weekend as the 2017 Charlottesville Attacks leaving one dead, the *Chicago Sun Times* reported that Chicago witnessed a slew of shootings, leaving nine dead and more than 30 injured. The shooters were black. Most of those dead and injured were black too. Chicago – a far larger and more liberal city than Charlottesville – didn't riot about the murders. This story didn't make it past the local news. #BlackLivesDontMatter to #BLM.

There are countless examples of more vandalism and injuries directly attributable to #BLM demonstrations than white nationalist rallies. Anyone who vandalizes, assaults or kills others – regardless of race or party – deserves to be chained to hay and shit on by pigs and chickens. These people are thugs – not the President, Mayor or County Commissioner.

The U.S. is the most racially diverse, tolerant country in the world. Lynchings are outliers. There are always isolated incidents.

The average American doesn't give a damn about white supremacists, the KKK or other racists. Nearly none of the people in the United States worship racist political leaders. Racist losers are in the tens of thousands – about the size of a small county. It took them decades to finally get the media coverage and a tiny ass group of less than 3,000 people to make headlines in Charlottesville. They are weak.

Compare that to the criminal ways of #BlackLivesMatter and Antifa rallies — millions of people have marched to date. They've left public and private properties destroyed, created tens of millions of dollars' worth of damage, killed tens of innocent civilians and police officers, and injured hundreds of people in the process. For the first time in my life, I heard fear in the voices of policemen I personally knew in the summer of 2016 because of a #BLM riot that intentionally killed five police officers in Dallas, Texas.

There is no comparison.

If digital liberals want Trump to declare "white nationalists" as "domestic terrorists," then he should also declare #BlackLivesMatter AND Antifa AND about 20 Muslim organizations as "domestic extremist terrorist organizations."

The problem is folks on both sides lump entire populations, generations, and races into labels.

The right to peaceably assemble is an important part of our *First Amendment* and *Bill of Rights*, but assembling for irrelevant causes that don't affect civil rights or people's well-beings, running people over with cars, creating chaos, and vandalizing public and private properties are what these "peaceable assemblies" have turned into. All participants are at fault here: #BlackLivesMatter, #WhiteLivesMatter, alt-rightists, alt-leftists, liberals, conservatives, white supremacists (I hate calling the peaceful ones "white supremacists" – all they want is what's best for their race, just like I want what's best for my race). They are immature, childish losers.

The delusional white advocates / supremacists say, "Jews will not replace us!"

What on Earth are they referring to?

Those Jews... always moving to the South and stealing the white man's jobs at the saloons and farms □*face palm*.

Meanwhile, Wall Street, the billionaire class, the corporations and the "globalists" are taking every last penny away from 99% of the rest of the country and laughing while they're' doing it... because people *choose* to protest immaterial issues they created or have little to do with.

If people had enough money to live without stress and the fear of unemployment, had their health care needs taken care of, and had sufficient funds or support for their retirement, then all bigotry, hatred, anger and racism would melt away.

It's all economic. The wealthy and elites have this status. They have it because they have captured the system.

To divert attention from the plunder of our labor, they pit the rest of the 99% against one another like animals. It's the classic divide and conquer strategy.

As we fight among ourselves and destroy what little we have left – our last freedoms – they loot and plunder and remain above the law.

We have to break this cycle, and it can be broken. It's all about money. Money is power.

A society so weak, so coddled, so needy of authoritarian protection in even the most insignificant aspects of their interaction with their fellow citizens destroys its own freedom.

People need to be more productive and find meaningful work and hobbies instead of whining, crying, killing, or destroying property, people or ideas that have nothing to do with the progression or improvement of their lives. They need to toughen up, get on with their lives, and stop vesting so much in stupid symbols. Symbols are not life.

152

Peace be with you.

Chapter 10

WHY TRUMP HAS NOTHING TO DO WITH RACISTS OR RACISM

Facebook Post:

"We have had racist hate crimes in my neighborhood. Some one painted Swastikas painted on two homes — one Indian and one Black family. There have been hate notes about sending Indian Doctors sent back to India."

The idiot thugs in this poster's neighborhood are at wrong. Anyone who is so inspired by President Donald Trump (his haters and lovers) to the point that they vandalize or assault others deserves to be chained to hay and shit on by pigs and chickens. The thugs are the real dunces — not the President or his advisors. The previous systems (not Administrations) have succeeded in producing such scummy people.

If illegal racism continues, then it is my hope all these people get caught and charged. We don't have a system like in other countries where people can just pay off the cops or legal bureaucrats.

Does this mean all Trump supporters are thugs who write hate letters to brown people? There are many upper-middle class Trump supporters who are solid citizens and live peaceful lives. There are many lower-middle class Trump supporters who do the same. You'll find such folks within the Indian, Mexican, and Muslim communities too.

I don't see freedom when fellow Indians are destroyed by fat idiot police officers... or their convenient stores or places of worship are raided for no reasons.

Does that mean I should also blame the country as a whole for such a problem?

The people who carry out such atrocities are idiots. Go after them... not the flag, monument, statue, national anthem or person who wrote the national anthem.

America is not violently racist. President Barack Obama never got a machete and chopped off a citizen's head... neither has Trump. They have never murdered or imprisoned anyone who's challenged the government.

At times, the suspects are some fat idiot cops or security. Other times, they're violent murderers who have no respect for human life. That doesn't mean the entire country is like this.

I just got back from a restaurant, and the white waitresses were really nice to me. When I go out tonight, I'll be on the lookout for some racist shit... since that's what digital liberals say this "country is on" and is all pervasive. I'll be sure to take videos and pictures too. It's everywhere.

NOT!

The American flag represents the embodiment of the LEAST amount of oppression IN THE WORLD. The importance of national anthem represents the act of coming together. Other countries copy our Constitution because of this powerful display.

When people stand for the national anthem, they don't do it to honor slavery or racism against blacks. They don't do it to honor Francis Scott Key.

The idea that the United States is "such a racist country" is incredibly far from the truth. Just look at other countries that are explicitly racist...

Japan Today reported that Japan's government practices what is called "positive discrimination," while displaying low tolerance for refugees and people from other countries. Nowhere in U.S. legislation is a term like "positive discrimination" used.

Rolling Stone reported that German neo-Nazis talk openly about anti-Semitic ideas. Sure, there are neo-Nazis everywhere, but in the U.S., such folks get zero or very negative coverage and are not accepted by society.

Salon reported that Israel has a long history of committing serious crimes against Israeli Arabs – completely innocent folks and many of whom aren't even Muslim. Again, such heinous acts happen everywhere, but they're few and far between in the U.S.

Wikipedia reports that in Pakistan – a majority Muslim nation – conflicts flare between Shiite and Sunni Muslims on a daily basis. Citizens kill fellow citizens and die. Most U.S. citizens don't even know the difference between Shiites and Sunnis.

And now to my Motherland: India...

White supremacist ideology is common in India, where lighter skin is glorified by the movie and advertising industries, among others...

Hindu gods and goddesses are white. Just look online at Brahma, his wife Saraswati, Lakshmi, Durga. They're not brown like most Indians.

White has been the dominant race to Indians. It's ingrained in our blood and psychology today. You can't change evolution or history.

Even children's books tell stories of the White Man bossing Indians around. He ruled the world. He was at the top. It started with Jungle Book. It ended with *The White Man's Burden*. Damn you Rudyard Kipling!

That's why it's OK to make fun of white people. "White Men Can't Jump." *White people can't dance.*

They're still superior in the eyes of the common Indian.

I went to India with a few white friends in 2016. We got hooked up with free shit – food, drinks, hash, tickets – and we were getting stopped every 15 minutes by random people – guys and girls – asking if they could take pictures with us. Why? Because we were a group with a bunch of white people (except me).

Growing up as a person of color, I viewed whites as elite. They sat courtside at the basketball games. They portrayed rich, powerful people in movies.

White girls were much prettier than any other types of girls in elementary school. I was too scared to talk to them... because they were white... and I was brown. The most upscale strip clubs are predominantly white.

Indian parents want their kids to get with the "fair-skinned" Indians – aka white Indians.

"My gosh! She is so fair!!!

"Gori gori gori." Hai.

Translation: She/he looks white. She/he is beautiful.

It's nearly every young Indian man's fantasy to get with a white chick at some point in his life – whether she's Indian (there are light-skinned Indians) or not. Hookups, hookers, girlfriends, strippers, secretaries, nurses... white white white.

I've heard the same applies to Indian girls' fantasies too.

That's White Power.

Do Browns hold that same power? I know I didn't grow up reading about *The Brown Man's Burden*.

On top of skin color, there is also discrimination between different regions and states within India. It's why so many North Indians are clueless about South India, and vice versa.

"He's Punjabi Sikh? Does his brain function properly? His wife probably cooks good food.

"He's South Indian? He's probably dark, lazy and prays and studies a lot.

And then there's the whole caste system and its impact on society...

The lower castes accept who they are. I'm talking about untouchables... the people who clean homes and cook food. And they're treated like inferiors... not poorly, but very few people in the U.S. would talk to such folks the way that untouchables in India are talked to.

Thanks Trump.

***

I'm astonished that it took a Donald Trump for so many digital liberals to recently realize that racism exists. Maybe I've just seen it more growing up in Texas and attending a 96% white high school.

It's hard to get a grasp of the people in the country when you live in socialist republics like New York, Maryland and California [where a bulk of the digital liberals referenced in this book reside(d)].

People need to stop taking offense to anything and everything. There's a reason why we laugh our asses off at racial jokes by stand-up comedians. Yet when a politician says much tamer stuff in real life, he or she is lynched.

My lawyer told me that on his first day of orientation at Cal Berkeley, students had sensitivity training. One of their case studies depicted Chris Rock as not funny because he's offensive.

Thank you, socialist government school Berkeley, for forcing your students to think what is funny and not funny...

Chris Rock is fuck*ng hilarious. Anyone who says he's offensive is a loser and can go cry to their mommy.

Digital liberals are responsible for Trump winning because they decided that other opinions and ways of looking at the world are unacceptable. If you call a digital liberal out on his or her baseless opinion or don't agree with them, then you're labeled a freak, evil, stupid idiot, racist, xenophobe, or deplorable.

How do you think people are going to vote if you talk to them like that?

The more digital liberals whine and cry, the more the "Silent 49%" will grow. The Silent 49% was so shamed that they let their votes do the talking.

Bringing facts to light doesn't justify being called a racist or bigot or Islamophobe... but unfortunately, that's the way digital liberals operate – and it's what propelled Trump to victory. The silent voters didn't want to be called names despite the facts, so they fought back with their votes.

Chapter 11
WHY SO MANY INDIAN AMERICANS SUPPORT DONALD TRUMP

Facebook Post:
"Trump's supporters are only white racists. I went to one of his rallies, and there was zero diversity."

Donald Trump held a rally in Tampa (where I live) three days before the 2016 Election, and there were too many Indians to count (it didn't hurt that Tampa's annual India Festival was taking place next door). At the same time, there were nearly 30,000 people in attendance total. It may have seemed like everyone in the crowd was white, but that rally showed that Trump has a minority of minorities.

People who attend political rallies are not an accurate representation of any candidate's voting base.

Republicans don't attract large amounts of people of color. This was a major issue for John McCain in 2008 and Mitt Romney in 2012.

The Hindu reported that more Indians voted for and donated to President Donald Trump than any other Republican candidate in history.

How did this happen? It's not that magnificent a feat if you dig into the numbers...

Indian immigrants are fiscally and socially very conservative in their lifestyles, yet more than 80% of them vote Democrat, which is a party that is fiscally and socially very liberal. The second generation in the West is far more liberal.

Al Jazeera reported that Barack Obama got 88% of the Indian vote in 2008 and 2012, so McCain and Romney had little Indian support. Furthermore, there were less than half as many Indians who could vote in 1988 when Bush Sr. won than the number of Indians who can vote today.

Trump's 2016 landslide also happens to be the most lopsided Republican victory in our lifetimes (Bush in 1988 was the last time a Republican cracked 300 Electoral Votes).

While Trump raised unprecedented Indian support among Republicans, it still pales in comparison fractionally to the support the Clintons and Obama have had within the community.

My close contacts with the Indian Republicans of Louisiana, Texas, New Jersey and New York ALL told me about Trump's high numbers of Indian supporters. It was far greater than both Bushes in 2004 and 1988.

The wealthy, upper-class Indians I know in Houston and Tampa were also majority pro-Trump. Most of these people were Bill Clinton voters and donors in the 90's and Obama voters in 2008.

The general trend is that Indian Trump supporters staunchly support Indian nationalist Prime Minister Narendra Modi. Indians who hate Modi share the same hatred for Trump. This does not mean that Modi supporters like Trump too.

In August 2016, I attended a lecture in Tampa by one of Indian Prime Minister Modi's top aides on entrepreneurship. He said the Indian Bharatiya Janata Party (BJP) consists of pro-business leaders who prefer Republicans over Democrats because Republicans are better for the Indian economy and because they take tougher stances against India's rival, Pakistan.

For example, the *Times of India* reported that Ronald Reagan played a crucial role in improving US-India relations by seeking India's help in science and technology, leading to the Indian dotcom and IT booms of the 90's.

It was also George W. Bush who signed the Civil Nuclear Agreement that grew India's economy by bringing in more than $150 billion in nuclear power revenue. Bush also lifted various economic sanctions imposed on India by President Bill Clinton's Administration.

During his campaign, Trump said he would cut cash flow to China and Pakistan and focus on improving India in the region.

Trump also has significant business interests in Delhi, Mumbai, Gurgaon, and a few other Indian cities.

The big elephant in the room is Islam. Trump's rhetoric against radical Islam got him a swarm of non-Muslim, Indian supporters.

Muslim violence against Hindus, Sikhs, Christians, Jews, Buddhists – pretty much every other religion – isn't a recent development. It dates back long before the Mughals ruled India.

Indians who grew up during the Partition of India saw the mass slaughter of millions of people. Without getting into the politics of the split and fighting, just know that anti-Muslim sentiment in India went way up. As a result, my generation of Indo-Americans grew up in households that educated us about how Indians died long ago and continue to die today. While we may not agree with such sentiment – a sentiment echoed by Trump more than any other American politician – our parents largely do.

In the age of Trump, what's the future of Indians in U.S. politics?

We now have our first Indian American (Tamil) in the U.S. Senate: Kamala Devi Harris (D-CA). She was raised a Hindu by her single mother in Canada.

We have our first Indian American (Punjabi) in a President's Cabinet: Nimrata "Nikki" Randhawa Haley (R-SC). She was raised a Sikh by her immigrant parents and serves as Ambassador to the United Nations.

Haley was previously the Governor of South Carolina – the first state to secede from the Union and a founding member of the Confederacy. Despite this, Haley was elected and re-elected as Congresswoman and Governor in landslide fashions – a testament to the evolution of voters in historically segregated states of racial sentiment.

Haley – a minority in race, color and sex – was voted Congresswoman and Governor in a state that – 150 years earlier – dictated citizens of color as 3/5ths a person and women as inhumane. The fact that Haley was elected to these high positions of office shows significant progress.

There's still Indo-American Congresswoman Tulsi Gabbard (D-HI). She was the only Democrat who spoke out against the Democratic National Committee (DNC) – where she was vice-chair – for holding so few debates and was the first Democrat to say that the DNC was rigging the primaries in favor of Hillary Clinton. She was scolded by DNC Chairwoman Debbie Wasserman Schultz and other bureaucrats at the time, whose political futures are now ruined after *WikiLeaks* published hacked emails that they actually did rig the debates and primaries. *The Gateway Pundit* reports that calls for Wasserman Schultz to testify in front of

Congress are increasingly growing because of her various scandals.

It's not just Indian Americans who have made strides in the Trump era. African-American neurosurgeon Dr. Ben Carson is now the Secretary of Housing and Urban Development (HUD). He grew up dirt poor in a one-bedroom inner-city Detroit apartment under the care of his single mother.

Trump also has Elaine Chao as his Secretary of Transportation. She is the first Asian American woman to be in a Presidential Cabinet.

The *Miami Herald* reports that Cuban-American Senator Marco Rubio (R-FL) continues to aid Trump in Latin American foreign policy initiatives.

Over the past year, Indian Americans and people of color are moving up in the political process. Voters and people in power are taking the necessary steps to reward minorities (including women) for their hard work.

The United States of America was founded as a Christian nation based on Christian principles. With Obama, Haley, Harris, Gabbard, Governor Bobby Jindal and others paving the way for immigrant children and people of color, it's only a matter of a few decades until a non-Christian makes bigger political waves.

None of this would be possible without the great democratic republic our Founding Fathers created and the open-mindedness and tolerance of many elected officials.

More than 230 years later, it is still a joy to watch democracy in action!

Chapter 12

HOW DONALD TRUMP COPIED PRESIDENTS BEFORE HIM TO BAN IMMIGRANTS FROM MUSLIM NATIONS

Facebook Post:

"Banning Muslim refugees from coming to our country is unprecedented. It is a total violation of human rights."

Truthfeed reports that Jimmy Carter, Bill Clinton, and Barack Obama all banned refugees from Muslim nations. There was no outrage from the Leftist news media because all three of the Presidents were Democrats.

In recent memory, Obama ordered a six-month Iraqi refugee ban in 2011, according to FOX News. Trump has a 90-120 day ban on immigrants from six countries (not Muslims) that the Obama Administration vetted, targeted and recommended, and the Leftist (social) media lost its mind.

Where was the outrage when Obama dropped over 26,000 bombs — as reported by *The Guardian* — on these same Middle Eastern countries in 2016 alone? I guess bombing innocent civilians in foreign countries 72 times a day keeps Americans on social media safer and happier than 90 day bans on refugees from these same countries.

Obama's Terrorist Travel Prevention Act of 2015 wasn't much different than Trump's Executive Order on refugee bans...

Obama's ban was on immigrants from seven Muslim nations that his Administration singled out and vetted – many of whom practice the worst of Sharia Law and persecute Christian minorities – and the same seven nations that Trump singled out as well. Digital liberals are unaware about laws based on Sharia. While learned people may know about female genital mutilation (FGM) and stoning, the average person has no clue that dogs are banned in Iran. They're all being executed one by one by shots of chemicals that eat away the insides of their bodies. Do any countries need immigrants who think like this? That is just another example of something that's "strange" in the name of Islam.

Trump's ban ended up being on six of these nations. There are millions of Christians in these nations who were subject to this ban too... so this was not a "Muslim ban" like the mainstream media made it out to be.

Trump's "Muslim ban" was also not as unpopular as the digital liberals and mainstream media claimed it to be. A Politico-Morning Consult poll found that six in 10 American voters supported the travel ban. In this same poll, only 14% opposed the legislation.

There are nearly 200 other countries in this world. Britain, Germany, Austria, Canada, Australia are just drops of countries in a pool that have open borders. People have options. Who said America is the place to go when in trouble? The United States is not a humanitarian organization and has no responsibility to take in people or care for the world. Despite this, the U.S. has done more for other countries and the world than any other country.

America is still a haven for immigrants, and it always will be regardless of how many 90-day refugee bans it tries to impose.

Not taking refugees and closing our borders doesn't mean we are "heartless" or "mean". I lock my doors every day and night. I don't lock them because I "hate" the people outside. I lock them because I LOVE the people INSIDE! The chances of someone breaking in are very slim... but keeping my doors unlocked is not a risk I want to take because I want to be safe.

When will Muslim men actually fight for their lands as Continental Army soldiers did for nearly a decade starting in the mid-1770's? Americans have even fought for Muslim land when Muslim men wouldn't.

Man up... pick up a weapon and take your countries back.

Chapter 13

IRRATIONAL OUTRAGE ON PAYING FOR THE MEXICAN WALL

Facebook Post:
"A 20% tariff on Mexican goods will kill consumers. Mexican products are already so cheap we will have to eat the cost and lose money every day."

This digital liberal says that a 20% tax will "kill" consumers because they "have to eat the cost." This is incorrect. Consumers cannot be "killed" when retail shopping in a free market economy like the United States because they have choices. If they feel they're getting ripped off, then they can just shop elsewhere for cheaper items.

The digital liberal then goes on to say, "Mexican products are already so cheap." So this individual says the product is "so cheap," yet a 20% increase in price will "kill consumers"?

A 20% U.S. tariff on Mexican goods to pay for the Wall would result in approximately 20% higher prices on those goods in the U.S. People in the U.S. would stop buying *Mexican goods* because they could get cheaper alternatives elsewhere. If people in the U.S. stop buying Mexican goods, then U.S. wholesalers will stop importing Mexican goods. It would be a waste of money and bad business for them to continue to do business with Mexico.

The original poster is someone who likely thinks Mexico's greatest exports are avocados and manual labor. Americans will not eat the cost of pricey Mexican products like cars, alcohol, electronics, machines, engines, pumps, bullion, medical supplies, minerals, oil, and fuels – the greatest Mexican exports to the U.S.

Let's take cars as an example: Volkswagens, Fords, Hondas, Nissans Chevrolet and Ram trucks are not Mexican cars, but many of their parts are manufactured and imported from Mexico... so it's not just Mexican companies that stand to lose in this deal – it's American, Japanese, and German companies too (there are countless other countries who will lose a lot with other products and industries). These cars are subject to the proposed 20% tariff.

A Volkswagen Beatle currently costs $30,000. A 20% increase would make it $36,000. That's a $6,000 price difference. There are plenty of comparable cars to the

Beatle that can be bought for $30,000, so a consumer would go with an alternative option. Paying a $6,000 premium on anything is not something even a one percenter would do.

A price hike on cars manufactured in Mexico would allow other countries – or even U.S. companies – to enter the marketplace and sell comparable products at lower prices. This is how Trump wants to bring back jobs and production to the U.S. This is how he wants to make America great again!

An import tariff will put Mexico in a deep shitter – far deeper than the $15-20 billion cost to build the Wall... and the other countries who trade or do business with Mexico – like Japan and Germany in the earlier car example – will pressure Mexico for screwing them over.

When Trump imposes a tariff on Mexican goods since Mexico won't pay for the Wall, the U.S. will crumple Mexico's economy and trade.

Chapter 14

WHY DONALD TRUMP IS THE FURTHEST THING FROM A SEXUAL ASSAULTER

Facebook Post:

"You are being toxic. I am not your mother. I have lost complete respect for you if you don't or won't accept that the actions he [Trump] is describing in that tape are sexual assault. HE WAS RECORDED ON FILM SAYING HE DOES THIS [sexual assault]. Grabbing someone by their genitals IS SEXUAL ASSAULT – no questions asked."

As usual with digital liberals, they attack their opponents with emotional insults and make bold generalizations instead of defending their positions with facts.

Donald Trump told Billy Bush on an Access Hollywood tape from 2005:

"I'm automatically attracted to beautiful [women] – I just start kissing them. It's like a magnet. Just kiss. I don't even wait. And when you're a star, they let you do it. You can do anything. Grab 'em by the pussy. You can do anything." – Donald Trump

Let's break Trump and the Facebook poster's quotes down...

"Grabbing someone by their genitals IS SEXUAL ASSAULT – no questions asked."

This poster – per her unwritten, broad, made-up, theoretical definition of sexual assault – is accusing every husband, boyfriend, one-night stander, random hookup, or boy toy of being sexual assaulters.

What she doesn't understand: **if there is consent, then there is no sexual assault**.

Trump said, "When you're a star, THEY [women] LET YOU DO IT. You can do anything."

This is called consent, because, "They let you do it." Therefore, **what Trump described – legally – is not sexual assault**.

If women are encouraging and cooperating in Trump's sexual advances – like his grabbing of their pu**ies ("vagina" for you naïve, innocent, clueless, or as the digital liberals would call it, "ignorant," readers) – because he's a "star" they wanted to please – as implied by his words "they let you do it" – then WHAT HE SAID ON THE TAPE would not constitute sexual assault.

However, if Trump said ON THE TAPE that women did not like his touching them, told him to stop and he kept "doing it," bitch-slapped him across the face, and kicked him in the ball sack, then this description would constitute sexual assault. There is no consent. Women would have fought back. The women could call the cops and press charges against him because they did not "let" him "do it."

But the preceding scenario is NOT what Trump discussed. It's a made-up hypothetical.

Saying something on a tape and having readily available proof are two separate issues. Trump is protected by free speech on the tape, so he could even say that he sold heroin on the streets as a teenager, and he wouldn't be prosecuted or labeled a drug dealer. Broadly speaking, people can say anything they want to the media, just like I can generally write anything I want as a member of the media.

"HE WAS RECORDED ON FILM SAYING HE DOES THIS [sexual assault]."

Trump never said on the tape, "I do sexual assault," or, "I'm a sexual assaulter." We've established that what Trump said on the tape is not sexual assault because of consent laws.

Chapter 15

WHY MELANIA TRUMP WILL MAKE AMERICAN WOMEN HOT AGAIN

Facebook Posts:

"We can all unite and agree this is the hottest first lady we've ever had, right?"

"Melania Trump has fake tits, fake tan, fake nose. All women look better than her...hands down."

Melania is an uneducated trophy wife, I could write a book about what shit role model that is as flotus."

I'm not sure how anyone can have anything against Melania Trump personally because she hasn't done or said anything. A bunch of digital liberals hate on Melania because she's Donald's wife and is more attractive than her haters.

People with little to no fulfillment or meaning in life tend to spend their energy hating others. It's a reflection of their own deep misery. It's also a sign of success for the person being hated on.

Why does Marilyn Monroe get away with sleeping around and posing nude with feminist liberals but Melania can't? The video of Bill Clinton gawking at her during Donald Trump's Inauguration says quite a lot about her looks.

There is no denying the fact that Melania is hot — although there are plenty of women (and digital liberal men) who refuse to acknowledge this, which is akin to denying that the Holocaust didn't happen.

The First Lady Melania Trump will set a fine example for women who want to look their best. Looks still matter regardless of what people say... just ask any single person.

Melania will affect the way women look and dress, just as Jackie Kennedy did in the 60's and 70's... or even just as Kim Kardashian, Brooke Shields, and Tyra Banks have affected women in the 90's and today.

Inc. reports that Kardashian makes hundreds of millions of dollars in revenue every year. That's a large market opportunity for Melania... just like there's been a market for Jackie Kennedy's fashion designs and outfits, which are still in business.

I wasn't around in the 60's or 70's, but the data shows that women took care of their bodies far better back then. The best way to test how well people take care of their bodies would be Body Mass Index (BMI). The most recent BMI results show the US as consistently #1 or #2 fattest country in the world. In the 60's and 70's, the U.S. wasn't even in the top five.

So, BOTH MEN AND WOMEN have not been taking care of their bodies in this country... but Melania will likely have a far greater impact on women than she will men.

Ben Bradlee wrote a 1964 book about John F. Kennedy called <u>THAT SPECIAL GRACE</u>. It's all about JFK's impact on society and culture, including content dedicated to his hairstyle, suits, physique, and speech. The book concludes that both JFK and his wife Jackie had such a profound effect on personal, social and cultural issues that society improved.

JFK was handsome and looked athletic. He was wealthy. He had a captivating wife and children and a very photogenic family.

What does this mean as it relates to President Donald Trump? The obvious signs point to comb overs becoming more accepted and in-style. Older men, maybe men in general – single or divorced – will have more confidence in themselves. They too will believe they can get a girl as pretty as Melania... and they will do what it takes to make that happen, trying to emulate Trump in the process: wear nice suits, make lots of money, start businesses, stand up with little fear. This is all on top of whatever policies, attitudes, feelings and accomplishments The Donald has.

But it also means Melania will be a role model for many women too... just like Michele Obama, Laura Bush, Barbara Bush, and Hillary Clinton have been role models in different ways during my lifetime...

Michele Obama had superior intellect and oratory skills.

Hillary had vision, perseverance and persistence.

The Bushes gave love, compassion and support.

Let's face it: with Melania, we won't get intellect. We won't get inspirational speeches.

But we will have an example of someone who is beautiful to look at while she nears the big 5-0. She takes care of her body. She stuck with her man when the mainstream didn't.

We will have to wait another three or four years to see what further cultural changes there are. Trump-branded businesses are already picking up. Merchandise sales of The Donald's daughter Ivanka are up more than 200% despite public boycotts. There is a new wave of enthusiasm in the Trump products.

Regardless, Melania Trump will have far-reaching impacts, for better or for worse.

Chapter 16

HOW POLITICS CAN DESTROY A WORKPLACE... OR STOCK

Mass E-mail:

"If you do not agree... then please reply to this email with your resignation because you have no place here." – Matt Maloney, Co-founder & CEO of Grubhub

After Trump won the Election of 2016, Grubhub co-founder & CEO Matt Maloney sent out a memo to his 1000+ employees saying Trump-supporting staff were not welcome and should resign because pro-Trump employees have "no place" in his company. In other words, Maloney implied that those who disagree with his political creed should, "reply to this email with your resignation.

To top it all off, Maloney said, "We do not tolerate hateful attitudes on our team," as if Trump supporters or voters are hateful, racist, xenophobic, or sexist, or support hate, racism, xenophobia or sexism. That's like someone accusing Maloney of being a racist or criminal or supporting racism or criminal activity because the candidate he supported – Hilary Clinton – incarcerated masses of blacks and illegally hid top-secret government e-mails from the FBI.

The results of Maloney's threat: Nobody resigned. Only 20% of the recipients replied to the CEO saying they supported his stance. The rest of the 80% were silent... most likely because they were scared.

Maloney was so delusional and close-minded that he completely neglected the fact that nearly 50% of all voters in the country supported Trump. Consequently, Grubhub's stock (NYSE: GRUB) tanked more than 15% within a week.

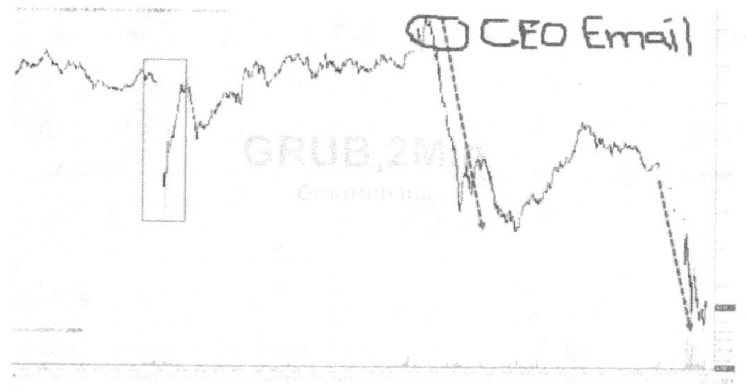

Maloney or the person below him hired every single person at Grubhub. If their employees are still employed, it's likely because they've been doing a good job. They've survived multiple layoffs and downsizing.

Senior management didn't ask whom employees voted for during the hiring process or while they've been working. Why did Maloney suddenly meddle with the personal lives of the people who work for him?

Just because a company donates to someone doesn't mean its employees approve of the donation. I spoke to a few of my friends and partners on Wall Street (banking side) after the Election, and it caught me by surprise how much Hillary Clinton was detested there, despite her family raising hundreds of millions of dollars from Wall Street over the course of their political and non-profit careers.

To all Grubhub's employees: If you voted for Donald Trump – in case you didn't already know – you may not feel welcome at Grubhub... because you are not welcome. I highly recommend you start searching for another job, because if you don't, you will forever work for a CEO who will be surrounded by controversy, instability and short-sellers who will try to bring his company down.

Chapter 17

WHY COLIN KAEPERNICK AND OTHER ATHLETES KNEELING DURING THE NATIONAL ANTHEM DOESN'T DO ANYTHING FOR ANYONE

Facebook Post:
"Congratulations to the NFL and its players for a message well sent to this country's demagogue-in-chief. Always remember that we as patriotic Americans are so much more than a flag or an anthem. #stopbigotry"

Protest and freedom of speech are protected by the *US Constitution*. These displays do more to ensure freedoms than anything else – certainly more than blind nationalism. In fact, the latter is not only dumb... it's absolutely dangerous and can lead to fascism or even dictatorship.

When you try to force/coerce people to do anything, they will do the opposite. It's only human nature.

Nevertheless, athletes protesting police brutalities against blacks by kneeling during the national anthem don't send messages or create change to any citizen, lawmaker or ideology outside of the for-profit news media, which blows the actions out of proportion so it can drive up its ratings.

According to *The Washington Post*, 737 people have been shot and killed by police through September 2017 in the United States. Of that number, there were 329 whites, 165 blacks, 112 Hispanics, 24 members of other races, and 107 people whose race was unknown. The vast majority of all these killings were justified homicides.

Indians in the United States get racially profiled by cops as illegal immigrants or potential terrorists. The reason you don't hear about rampant #BrownLivesMatter is because we don't "Fuck tha Police," as made popular by 80's and 90's rap group N.W.A.

If you want to fuck with the police, then the police will shoot you.

If "Americans are so much more than a flag or anthem," then what's the point in kneeling or refusing to honor the *Star-Spangled Banner?* There is no point.

The problem is not white-on-black crime or police brutalities in the hood. These are isolated and infrequent incidents. America does not suffer from a pandemic of white men going into ghettos shooting up black people.

Black-on-black crime occurs every day in some cities and nearly every hour nationwide.

Instead of plotting useless national anthem protests at state-of-the-art stadiums in front of tens of thousands of people, fix the issues in your own neighborhoods. No sane people have problems because of a national anthem or flag.

Kneeling during the national anthem is not going to appease anyone. After the kneels, players will demand something else.

Digital liberals are proud of kneels and dishonoring the country, but they don't understand that these actions create more division. Nothing is accomplished.

Former San Francisco 49ers quarterback Colin Kaepernick started this wave of stupidity. This is a man who wore a Fidel Castro t-shirt to a press conference while lamenting oppression and injustice in the United States. To make matters worse, the shirt had the caption, "Like minds think alike."

Image via CNN

Fidel Castro imprisoned and tortured hundreds and thousands of people to keep himself in power. The United States cut off diplomatic relations with Cuba because of the terrible things Cuba did under Castro's reign.

Nobody can do all bad. Castro had some great qualities... like implementing an education system with a 97% literacy rate, making it nearly impossible for kids to drop out of school. His communist approach also created one of the most honest and efficient healthcare systems in the world, with superior quality of care and little "junk food."

But most Cubans don't speak English, which is effectively banned in Cuban curricula. The people who do speak English – the smartest of the bunch – work in restaurants or hotels. They grow up aspiring to be waiters.

What's the point of being "literate" when you can't even speak the world's reserve language? They don't teach or speak French, Arabic, or Mandarin either.

On top of that, there is virtually no Internet in Cuba. Citizens don't know how to operate basic computers, Apples, Windows, or Office.

If and when relations with Cuba open up globally, its workforce will struggle to work white collar jobs despite their superior "literacy" credentials.

Great job, Fidel!

Castro has been internationally touted as oppressive, murderous, and a violator of basic human rights.

North Korea's Kim Jong-un spends a lot of money on projects "to keep North Koreans happy." Does that mean people like Colin Kaepernick should be wearing Kim Jong-un t-shirts?

Hitler stood up for the lower and middle classes in Germany. Che Guevara did the same in Argentina.

All these people were loved in their countries.

If Kaepernick had dictators like the Castros for 57 years in power, he would know what it's really like to be oppressed. Kaepernick has no understanding of history or politics.

If Kaepernick wants to contextualize oppressive dictators, then he should contextualize the great life and freedoms he and all Americans have instead of focusing on an issue that isn't even in the top five list of most important issues citizens care about. If #BlackLivesMatter means so much to him, then there are other ways to tackle the problem and provide solutions as opposed to just blaming the country as a whole. That does nobody any justice.

I don't see freedom when a handful of fellow Indians are assaulted by fat idiot police officers... or their convenient stores or places of worship are raided for no reasons.

Does that mean I should also blame the country as a whole for such a problem?

The people who carry out such atrocities are idiots. Go after them individually... not the flag or national anthem or person who wrote the national anthem.

America is not violently racist. President Barack Obama never got a machete and chopped off a citizens' head. He has never murdered or imprisoned anyone who's challenged the government. The same goes for President Donald Trump.

The suspects in #BlackLivesMatter are dumb cops or security. That doesn't mean the entire country is like them.

The solution to #BlackLivesMatter: police hiring standards need to be overhauled. There are too many smart people on the sidelines, as evidenced by the latest unemployment reports. It's only going to get worse. Go to better schools to recruit cops and security. Stop recruiting out-of-shape, college dropout GEDs to police our streets.

As I write this, I just got back from a restaurant, and the white waitresses were really nice to me. When I go out tonight, I'll be on the lookout for some racist shit... since that's what this country is on and is all pervasive. I'll be sure to take videos and pictures too. It's everywhere.

NOT!

The American flag represents the embodiment of the LEAST amount of oppression IN THE WORLD. The importance of national anthem represents the act of coming together. Other countries copy our Constitution because of this powerful display.

When people stand for the national anthem, they don't do it to honor slavery or racism against blacks. They don't do it to honor Francis Scott Key.

If Kaepernick and his fellow athletes aren't standing because of these reasons, then they should've never stood for it to begin with and should be calling for a replacement of the Anthem. Anyone with moral and intellectual clarity will recognize that America is not perfect.

Most professional athletes are cheaters. They played in the NCAA, which is about bribing players and families with cash, sneakers, hookers, and strippers. No wonder they kneel in the NFL... they have turned into spoiled brats who could be entitled criminals.

Many of these athletes have no clue what they're kneeling about. The University of North Carolina academic-athletic scandal uncovered that a bulk of college and professional athletes read and write like fifth graders.

CNN reports:

> Early in her career as a learning specialist, Mary Willingham was in her office when a basketball player at the University of North Carolina walked in looking for help with his classwork.
>
> He couldn't read or write.
>
> "And I kind of panicked. What do you do with that?" she said, recalling the meeting.
>
> Willingham's job was to help athletes who weren't quite ready academically for the work required at UNC at Chapel Hill, one of the country's top public universities.
>
> But she was shocked that one couldn't read. And then she found he was not an anomaly.
>
> Soon, she'd meet a student-athlete who couldn't read multisyllabic words. She had to teach him to sound out Wis-con-sin, as kids do in elementary school.

And then another came with this request: "If I could teach him to read well enough so he could read about himself in the news, because that was something really important to him," Willingham said.

After President Trump uninvited the Golden State Warriors basketball team from vising the White House because their players publicly stated they weren't going to show any signs of support for Trump, basketball great Lebron James Tweeted:

> U bum @StephenCurry30 already said he ain't going! So therefore ain't no invite. Going to White House was a great honor until you showed up!

There are so many errors with this message, and it shows a lack of education and literacy even at the pinnacle of professional sports.

Some of these players have publicly stated that they are being treated as slaves by their employers. You can't make millions of dollars per year as a slave. If professional athletes are slaves, then sign me up to be a slave too. I have no problem living in big, fancy houses and driving Bugattis and Bentleys.

Where was Kaepernick's political talk when he was a rising star?

Why did he wait until after his crappy preseason to start discussing the atrocities black people face in the US?

You really think it's a coincidence that he went from blandly apolitical to staging a headline-dominating political protest around the time he realized his lucrative professional football career was coming to an end?

Kaepernick is a spoiled young man who divides rather than unites. While African Americans comprise a huge portion of the NFL, the league's viewing audience exhibits more diversity. Kaepernick makes many non-black viewers feel like they're some sort of oppressive racists since they love this country and are not black, unlike him. There are billions of issues at hand. Kaepernick's malcontent on one issue doesn't justify his divisive actions for a country, its flag or national anthem as a whole.

There are countless professional sports owners who've publicly backed Trump. These are the people who employ professional athletes. The last thing these owners want is for sponsors to leave, ratings to plummet or ticket sales to dwindle. Unsurprisingly, this is what has happened to the NFL as a result of these silent protests. Playing politics is financial suicide for any apolitical business. It will ultimately lead to downsizes in team staffs and less money for player contracts.

Yes, the players are responsible for making less money.

Can you imagine a heart surgeon kneeling / protesting some random issue in front of an apprehensive patient before surgery?

Businesses are not political action committees. The NFL and each franchise within it operate as businesses.

Employees and contractors should behave according to the rules of their bosses. If they don't, they get fired.

By not standing for the national anthem and disrespecting the US flag, Kaepernick is overshadowing the overarching great things the US provides and stands for. Kaepernick is not voicing an opinion. He's executing an action that shows he doesn't like this country... and if he doesn't like the US, then he should get out. He should give back all the money he's made thanks to this country. He should give back his cars, girls, bottles, parties and freedoms. He should denounce the education, culture and fun he's partaken in.

Here's a man with a 100+ pound turtle living in his backyard. Good luck transporting and taking care of that in Cuba!

Photo via Twitter/@BryanAGraham

By leaving the country, he'll be happier. It's a great solution to his problem.

For example, I hated living in Baltimore during my mid-20's. What did I do? I got the hell out of there. I now live in Florida. If I start hating Florida, then I'll just pack my bags and go down to South America. There is nothing un-American about being happy by moving to another country.

Nobody is "telling" Kaepernick and fellow kneelers to leave in a forceful way. People are just saying they'd be happier in another country. It's a valid solution to their problems.

I have plenty of friends who hated the U.S. and left the country for good. They didn't like how the U.S. treated their businesses, paychecks, health, or healthcare. These were middle class individuals with families and kids. If they can do it, professional athletes worth tens of millions of dollars can do it too.

Kaepernick's crappy play forced him out of the league. His team, the San Francisco 49ers, combined for seven wins in 2015 and 2016 – one of the worst records during that two-year span.

Kaepernick will be forced to play in Canada – far more "racist" a country than the US, according to *Maclean's*.

Chapter 18

WHY NBA COACHES GREGG POPOVICH, STEVE KERR, AND STAN VAN GUNDY SHOULD SHUT THEIR MOUTHS ABOUT POLITICS

"The whole process has left all of us I think feeling disgusted and disappointed." – Steve Kerr, Head coach of the Golden State Warriors & Seven-time NBA Champion

"I'm just sick to my stomach. Not basically because the Republicans won or anything, but the disgusting tenor and tone and all of the comments that have been xenophobic, homophobic, racist, misogynistic. I live in that country where half of the people ignored all of that to elect someone. That's the scariest part of the whole thing to me. It's got nothing to do with the environment and Obamacare, and all of the other stuff." – Gregg Popovich, Five-time NBA Champion while serving as President of Basketball Operations & Head coach of the San Antonio Spurs

"I don't think anybody can deny this guy is openly and brazenly racist and misogynistic and ethnic-centric. I don't know how you go about it, if you're a person of color today or a Latino. Because white society just said to you, again—not like we haven't forever—but again, and emphatically, that I don't think you deserve equality. We don't think you deserve respect. And the

same with women. That's what we say today, as a country. We should be ashamed for what we stand for as the United States today... Our society has said, 'No, we think you should be second-class citizens. We want you to be second-class citizens.'" – Stan Van Gundy, President of Basketball Operations & Head coach of the Detroit Pistons

Before I question and criticize three of my favorite (and easily top seven) coaches in the NBA, I'd like to share my background in sports...

I attended two leading basketball universities – Duke and Syracuse. Syracuse boasts one of the best broadcast and digital journalism programs in the world, and I got a chance to cover sports topics, including the men's basketball team and the controversies that have surrounded it.

For two summers, I interned as a basketball operations draft evaluator for former Philadelphia 76ers President of Basketball Operations & General Manager Sam Hinkie while he was Senior Vice President of Basketball Operations with the Houston Rockets. I also interned for the Houston Astros eons ago.

I got my internship with the Houston Rockets because Stan Van Gundy's brother – current ABC / ESPN Sports analyst and then head coach Jeff Van Gundy – handpicked me to receive season tickets to serve as a Houston Rockets Red Rowdy during my senior year of high school. I tried out to win those tickets. The experience got my foot in the door within the Rockets organization.

I still have very deep contacts and connections in sports that run through players, managers, agents and coaches – both collegiately and professionally.

Famous People are out of Touch with Reality

I'm putting Steve Kerr, Gregg Popovich, and Stan Van Gundy under the microscope because I follow their successes and commentary...

Kerr and Popovich are extremely well-versed on many issues – far more than others in their profession – but their statements show they know little about how out of touch they are with reality and how the actual political process works...

Kerr's father served as President of the American University of Beirut and was assassinated by two

Islamist Jihadist gunmen in 1984. Popovich served in the U.S. Air Force Academy and served five years of required active duty, during which he toured Eastern Europe and the Soviet Union.

These coaches don't understand the bullying they are doing to their colleagues, players, and fans when they take political stances. For them to think that *everyone* they know is "feeling disgusted and disappointed" and didn't vote for Donald Trump is extremely narrow-minded, especially when the data shows otherwise...

For some reason, the liberals think Trump voters or supporters don't exist or are few and far in between. If that were the case, then Trump would've never made it out of the primaries. Real, living, breathing people wouldn't have bothered registering and showing up to the booths.

That's not how a democracy works.

Liberals don't understand that 49% – nearly 1 out of 2 people – voted for TRUMP. That means half of all voters took the time and effort to register and get their asses to the booths to punch their ballots for Trump to be President of the United States.

<u>Heavy reports</u> that 43% of people in the US who were eligible to vote didn't register or, if they did, they didn't end up voting. This is likely because they have no problem with Trump or his policies. If they did have problems with him, then they would have voted against him.

The data shows that Trump won in states with higher rates of voter turnouts... so the people in the country supporting him should actually be higher – more like 50% or 51% Trump support if more people voted.

People who didn't vote at all (like me) don't necessarily hate Trump. They don't necessarily hate Hillary. They don't necessarily love Trump either... and they don't love Hillary. If they felt any one way about either candidate, then they would've voted... but they didn't.

A *majority* of the House of Representatives and a *majority* of Senate support Donald Trump. These are officials who were elected by real, living, breathing people – the same people who pay for basketball tickets or work in NBA front offices. A majority of the Electoral College – the body that determines Presidential nominations and overall winners – supports him too.

The Trump movement was not tiny. It was a group effort of nearly half the country. A small subset of the population did not do this. More people voted in the 2016 Election than in any other Election ever before. Trump got THE MOST ELECTORAL VOTES OF ANY REPUBLICAN NOMINEE since 1988, and he got THE MOST POPULAR VOTES OF ANY REPUBLICAN NOMINEE EVER. That's a lot of people who VOTED for him.

There are too many opinions out there and not enough realism or acceptance of 21st century trends and affairs. These elitist, multimillionaire coaches need to look at the data and accept that one out of two people they stop on the street will have no issues with Trump. It's surprising that all three coaches live in or have spent considerable time in Texas, Arizona, Michigan and Florida, yet they acted so surprised after the results came out.

Trump supporters are everywhere. They're just in the closet because people like Kerr, Popovich, and Van Gundy shame and shun them.

There are countless professional sports owners who've publicly backed Trump... and my sources within the sports and entertainment industries have also told me that a wide group of players don't feel welcome to share their political views because of comments made from the likes of Kerr, Popovich and Van Gundy. People whom these coaches meet and work with every day voted for Trump. Just because they voted for him does not mean they are bad people or that they deserve to be treated differently. It sure as hell doesn't mean they're "racist," "misogynistic," "homophobic" or "xenophobic." People have millions of reasons to vote. I could easily say whomever voted for Hillary Clinton believes in colluding with Wall Street, media (evidenced by the removal of Debbie Wasserman Schultz as Chair of the DNC), corporatists (look at her donations), and terrorist nations (Clinton Foundation donations to countries funding terrorism and her incompetence as Secretary of State), which would make the voters crooks and terrorists themselves. They would also believe in using their spouses for political gains despite the spouse's repeated affairs and sexual assault accusations. Therefore, they believe in the righteousness of sexual assault and are sexual assaulters.

Oh yeah, and Hillary stuck with her top aide Huma Abedin, who was going to be her Chief of Staff. *The Hill* reported that Abedin's family has ties to the Muslim Brotherhood, and her husband is under investigation for child pedophilia. So, because Hillary supports such a woman, that means her voters support child pedophilia too.

But I would never use such illogic in arguments or as defenses because they are baseless conjectures of thought.

The coaches may have the defense: "Well my players and colleagues all hate Trump. They told me so." But that's exactly the line of thinking that got Trump elected in the first place – a silent 49% who did the talking with their votes – because they had no other recourse to fight back. They were too ashamed to tell the truth to their friends, families, employers, polling agencies, and the like.

Too many of these multimillionaire celebrities live in their own bubble and refuse to acknowledge other sides of opinion once they've made up their mind on surface issues. The coaches – like masses of digital liberals – harp on nebulous trigger words like, "racist," "homophobic," "xenophobic."

I've praised Kerr and Popovich for having the knowledge to speak generally, but Van Gundy blindly states, "I don't know how you go about it, if you're a person of color today or a Latino. Because white society just said to you, again—not like we haven't forever—but again, and emphatically, that I don't think you deserve equality. We don't think you deserve respect. And the same with women. That's what we say today, as a country."

If Van Gundy wants to talk race, then why does he have no idea that President Obama contributed to the rise of black unemployment, college dropout, homicide and incarceration rates while he was in office? There is nothing more unequal to blacks than that.

If we're going to be honest about the failings of one President, we must also be honest about the failings of the other...

Newsmax reports that, by nearly every economic indicator, blacks (majority of NBA players) were worse off at the end of President Obama's Presidency than when he was sworn into office. During Obama's terms, black Americans experienced record lows in small business loans and saw their lowest homeownership rates in 25 years. This is along with having record highs in unemployment and experiencing large amounts of wealth loss. Since Obama took office, the racial wealth gap grew more than 30%.

Obama was a great President for white people... but the data shows he did little to help the African-American community in a significant way. It makes no sense to allow shootings and murders in black inner cities to keep rising while still making sure the "lily-white" suburbs Van Gundy has lived in stay safe. Trump has publicly Tweeted he wants to make streets safer for innocent black folk. If he tries doing that, he'd be doing more for the black community than any other President since the 1960's.

In February 2017, *Reuters* reported that President Trump signed a measure to boost government support for the nation's historically black colleges (HBCUs). Trump's order moved the federal government's program for promoting HBCUs back under direct oversight of the White House.

Historically black colleges and universities (HBCUs) took huge steps backward under President Obama. Enrollment dropped significantly, and more than $170 million in funding was tossed down the drain.

It's rather tragic that President Trump has already done more for historically black colleges and universities than President Barack Obama did. This is the fault of the

Obama Administration for setting the standard so low in the first place.

Many of the people yelling and screaming about what Trump isn't doing for black people should have been doing so during Obama's presidency. Do-nothing politicians continue to scam citizens. Wait, scratch that... they do nothing for black people, but do lots of things for the rest of America. Most politicians – while they will ignore reparations – also pay little attention to urban violence, allow black unemployment to fester, and do nothing to save horrible schools.

Democrats own a monopoly of control in major American inner cities – all the "killing fields" like Chicago, Detroit (where Van Gundy lives), Baltimore, New Orleans and St. Louis. Democrats own these inner cities and have owned them for decades. Deep blue states run by liberal Democrats are going broke all over the United States. You can add Connecticut and socialist California to that list, per *Forbes* and *The Mercury News*. Democrats and progressives are largely responsible for much of what is wrong with the inner cities and many oppressions black people and other minorities suffer. The Democrats continue to make the black community easy prey because they know they'll get most of their votes without doing anything to help.

Trump, on the other hand, has already made building up Black America a priority, calling for a "New Deal for Black America."

If Van Gundy wants to talk more about racial facts, then look no further than the Clintons, who have incarcerated more blacks than any other political family. That's quite a feat considering the Kennedys were around pre-civil rights and for a much longer time. The Daily Beast reported that the Clintons have incarcerated more blacks than any other family this country has witnessed. There's only been two of them who've been around for four decades post-Civil Rights. The Kennedys, on the other hand, have been around far longer with a lot more people pre-Civil Rights... and the Clintons have still persecuted more blacks.

"I signed a bill that made the problem worse," Hillary Clinton said about black incarceration in July 2016.

Bill and Hillary have been true masters of deception. Coaches like Van Gundy can say whatever they want, but that's a horrible history of race relations based on what the Clintons have done.

There are Trump supporters who are uneducated racist hillbillies. That's a fact. There's no denying racist Trump supporters like there's no denying there were racist Gary Johnson and Hillary Clinton supporters.

But there are countless Trump supporters who are not racist...

They like Trump's strategy to defeat ISIS. They favor lower taxes. They want the borders protected. They like that he's anti-establishment and a disruption to the status quo and political elite.

They are great people who have changed many lives, including mine. The CEOs of more than half my clients support him (many of whom are minorities). I hang out or talk to Trump supporters every day. They are a part of nearly half of the country supporting him. These are tech executives, Wall Street traders, entrepreneurs, blacks, Indians, Muslims, etc.

Want to see which of your friends support Trump? Just go to his Facebook Fan Page. You can see which of your friends "Like" him. If digital liberals were more open and tolerant, then they too would understand that pro-Trump people are all around them – including on Facebook.

Those who profess to support tolerance and equality have become the most intolerant and chauvinistic.

There aren't enough racists or white supremacists to make enough of a political difference on a federal level. If there were, then Barack Obama would've never become President. He wouldn't have even made it past the primaries... and George Wallace and KKK Imperial Wizard David Duke would've been elected President.

There are people who voted twice for Obama in 2008 and 2012 yet voted for Trump in 2016. Racism cannot be the reason for this. Such people are not racist.

There are also white supremacist racists who voted against Obama – nearly 100% – twice in 2008 and 2012 because of his half black skin color. The results show that their votes didn't matter, for Obama still won in landslides.

What does this all mean?

Again, there just aren't enough racist white supremacists to swing an Election.

Racial and identity politics will never be a winning strategy. Obama didn't use it in his campaigns, and he didn't use it against his opponents either.

Digital liberals and celebrities focus too hard on identity politics, which only a tiny segment of the country gives a sh*t about.

When it comes to jobs or the economy, these celebrities have nothing. They shill for corporate America, which is transforming by the month because of the digitization of business and outsourcing.

These coaches and celebrities are clueless that the last two Democratic presidents – Bill Clinton and Barack Obama – along with the entire Democratic Party leadership sold out their historic constituency: the working class.

Here's much of what killed the working class over the past 10 years:

-   Wall Street deregulation
-   Trillion-dollar bank bailouts after these institutions nearly destroyed the global economy and after committing fraud after fraud after fraud without anyone ever going to jail

- Letting homeowners go down the tubes with no bailouts, resulting in them losing their homes
- A trillion-dollar giveaway to insurance companies and then allowing them to dictate our healthcare

If the Democrats and digital liberals don't understand this, which it appears they don't, then they shouldn't hold power at all. That's why they keep losing.

Despite Trump's low status with the mainstream media and celebrities, his haters still can't win. Their losses are mounting up in Senate and Congressional runoffs and in 2017 gubernatorial and mayoral races.

Racial identity politics divided the Democrats and fringe voters in the Election of 2016, and it will be the downfall of the Democratic Party if it continues.

Popovich has said repeatedly he "can't really believe anything that comes out of his [Trump's] mouth." If Trump irks Popovich so much, then just vote him out in four years. Four years is a very short amount of time in the political process. Stop whining like a First World teenager.

The Real Cons

If Popovich and Kerr want to allude to Trump being a con politician, then they need to look at their own organizations and themselves for legitimately scamming their paying fans when they repeatedly rest their star players for no good reason...

The NBA and its teams market their star players. Fans pay hundreds of dollars for tickets to games – many times months in advance – to watch their favorite stars, and a few hours before tipoff, Popovich and Kerr announce they will sit their star players because "they need rest." This is a classic bait-and-switch in business without notice. By doing this, teams aren't putting out their full products to fans, who've already paid. The teams should give partial refunds or credits for their deliberate inability to deliver.

In my own small businesses, when customers or clients pay for a product or service, I can't respond back to them by saying, "Sorry, this year has been really grueling. I'll keep your money and deliver the work when I feel like it."

I know what it feels like to be ripped off. It's a big problem, and if I were one of these fans, I'd call my credit card company and ask them to void all charges for the tickets. I'd then report the franchise to the Better

Business Bureau and write on *Ripoff Report* how these coaches conned me.

It's only a matter of time until a class action lawsuit is filed. All it would take is a string of bad seasons to make fans unhappy.

I'm going to finish this chapter with some commentary from a Latina doctor. Her response is really all Coach Kerr, Popovich and Van Gundy need to read to understand their own intolerance and myopia.

Facebook Post:

"I was a silent trump voter like the majority of our country because I feared being bullied by the outspoken Hillary supporters. I feared being called a bully, racist, a hater, antiwoman, antigay, deplorable, anti-LOVE (are you kidding me?). If you really KNOW me you know that I am none of those things. I am an intelligent educated US citizen who believes in our democracy and wants to see the best for our country and believes that Trump was and is the best candidate we had for the job to build a safer and stronger USA. I would love to see a woman president-but I could not allow this country's first female president to be a corrupt criminal who would have socialized this country — we can do better. The American people have spoken and I hope that everyone in this country can respect our democracy and pull together to

make America great again. I think it is sad that people threaten cause they didn't get their way they are leaving this country, if you think that any country is better and stronger than USA and you can't respect the American people's vote this country might be better without you. Where is this love that democrats talked so much about ? I respected the opinion of all my democratic friends and I hope they will do the same for me. I am tired of being bullied and afraid to voice my opinion. I want to show my support for the president of the United States, Donald Trump. I wish everyone would Stop being so negative and support your country's decision. #silentnomore #stopthebullying #makeamericagreatagain #thepeoplehavespoken #trumptrainhasarrived #trump2016 #Notosocialism #nomasmantengo #saferUSA #strongerUSA #practicewhatyoupreach"

Chapter 19

WHY MERYL STREEP, GEORGE CLOONEY, LEONARDO DICAPRIO, AND HOLLYWOOD SHOULD SHUT THEIR MOUTHS ABOUT POLITICS

"'When was the last time an actor assassinated a president?"-
Johnny Depp

This chapter picks up where the last chapter left off. Hollywood celebrities are no different than rich, snooty high-profile coaches Steve Kerr, Gregg Popovich and Stan Van Gundy. You could replace the word "coaches" in the previous chapter with "Hollywood," and the same intentions and messaging would apply.

Actors and actresses are entertainers. Learned people know they have special interests in politics, philanthropy, and altruism. The public also knows how dysfunctional their family and personal lives are.

Hollywood elites are no different than most left-wingers, who only see what's on the surface and have little experience on issues they are passionate about. They speak from emotion rather than from facts or reality.

Hollywood's arrogance and self-importance are on display every year at awards shows like the Oscars and Golden Globes. Hollywood elites get on stage and think they promote good causes they know nothing about. It's why Leonardo DiCRAPrio flies private, fuel-wasting jets and yachts to teleprompted, six-figure speeches he gives on climate change, as reported by every celebrity tabloid imaginable. Celebrity lifestyles diminish their moral authority to lecture others on geopolitics, diversity, language, carbon emissions, and any other topic they don't understand.

Meryl Streep's 2017 Golden Globes anti-Trump speech was why Trump won the Election in the first place. All she needed to do was accept her award, thank a few people nobody except her knows, and get off stage. Instead, she went on a rant and encouraged the mainstream media to continue their misreporting and hidden agendas: the same strategy that got Trump elected, as explained throughout this book. Hollywood should have gotten the message that the mass aren't their sheep after Trump got elected.

In 2011, Streep played Margaret Thatcher in *The Iron Lady*, and Streep publicly supported Thatcher – arguably the closest female leader to Trump's politics in history.

How clueless can Streep be? She is a hypocrite and Marxist: blind, deaf and dumb. She is American-hating. America and capitalism are why she is wealthy and famous.

She asked the audience during her Golden Globe speech, "What is Hollywood?"

The answer is simple: it's where a bunch of overpaid and egotistical people get to play pretend and preach to the rest of us how to behave. Hollywood actors and actresses are children who never grew up. They earn so much money and privilege for reading lines someone else wrote. Very few of them have had real jobs that provide or create value.

Streep not only disparaged Trump. She offended athletes and MMA fighters too.

"Hollywood is crawling with outsiders and foreigners," Streep said. "If we kick them all out, you'll have nothing to watch but football and mixed martial arts, which are not the arts."

Streep's notion of consumerism is inaccurate...

People watch movies and shows that are promoted well by studios, critics and their peers... not because of the foreign actors and actresses in the films – and they watch movies and awards shows to break away from world problems.

Furthermore, Hollywood has extremely strict employment laws that prevent illegal aliens and terrorists from working.

There are LOTS of talented American actors. It's why making a long-lasting career in Hollywood is nearly impossible. Competition is heavy, and the shelf-lives of careers are short. Therefore, Hollywood would do just fine without a single "foreigner," if it ever reached that point, which it never will. The topic Streep brings up is hypothetical and moot.

Awards shows are fake, scripted marketing events for the most entrenched interests in Hollywood. For every winner, there are hundreds of others equally talented but less lucky and far less connected. It has little to do with finding and recognizing talent. The subjective selection process of recognizing talent is rigged.

George Clooney is another clueless, hypocritical Hollywood elitist. *People* magazine reported he has derided and criticized Trump on his tight immigration stances. Yet the *Hollywood Reporter* reported that Clooney the fraud has a wall around his mansion. Despite this, Clooney complained that media photographers jumped over his wall to take pictures of his twin children.

"Over the last week, photographers from *Voici* magazine scaled our fence, climbed our tree, and illegally took pictures of our infants inside our home," George Clooney said in a statement. "Make no mistake... the photographers, the agency and the magazine will be prosecuted to the full extent of the law."

Isn't that just too bad? Here is another Hollywood ignoramus criticizing the President for building a wall to keep illegals out, yet he is upset and says it is illegal for people to jump his own wall that he built. *Voici* should give out his address and send the entire illegal alien population of Mexico over Clooney's wall.

Good luck, Hollywood hypocrites!

Chapter 20

5 WAYS TO DEFEAT TRUMP IN 2020

Facebook Post:

"I urge my white friends to skip Thanksgiving this year to avoid sexist, racist, xenophobic, Islamophobic, homophobic, anti-Semitic relatives who voted for Donald Trump. These people are biased hypocrites. If they claim they aren't and that they voted for other reasons, ask them on the phone why they don't care enough about these issues. Let people know you refuse to tolerate hate speech and bigotry. We don't need your safety pins. We need your voice and actions now more than ever."

I've explained how digital liberals elected Donald Trump as President of the United States...

What does this mean for 2020?

There is good news for digital liberals: they can defeat President Donald Trump in 2020. Whining, complaining, arguing, and name-calling didn't work in 2016, and it will never work in any national referendum.

The strategy to defeat Trump is five-fold, and it's based on fatal flaws displayed by digital liberals:

1. Forgiveness

There is no healthy marriage, family, friendship or life without forgiveness – a crucial action to emotional health and spiritual survival. While sorrow produces pain, forgiveness brings joy and vitalizes the soul by cleaning the mind and liberating the heart.

People who don't forgive become a theater of conflict and bastion of grievances. They have no peace of soul and become sick mentally, physically, emotionally and spiritually.

President Trump made some questionable statements that got under the skin of his opponents... but that was all for show to get votes. He got what he needed.

The first step to change tomorrow is by forgiving today.

2. Acceptance

Anti-Trump hysteria has separated digital liberals from reality. If this continues, then the liberals as a whole (Democrats) won't make the political and policy adjustments that would win back the constituencies they lost.

Trump is the President of the United States, whether digital liberals like it or not. It is what it is.

Recounts, public tax records, and Russian hacking accusations won't change that. The votes are tallied. Trump and his businesses have been audited. He is here to stay.

3.   Love and understand thy neighbors

Social networks like Facebook are algorithmically controlled echo chambers that profit from confirmation bias. This is where people "socialize" with other people who think mostly like one another while getting "news" that is specifically geared toward similar tastes. Users get force-fed what they already want to hear.

Instead of connecting everyone, digital media has distorted the reality of the world. The Information Age has created technologies designed to connect and inform us, but the effect has been the opposite of intention.

If digital liberals want to connect with the world and better understand what's going on, then they need to get away from the echo chamber. They must do something without breaking any laws or violating human rights even if it makes them puke. They must watch or listen to uncomfortable content even if it makes them want to throw a brick into the TV set or iOS Podcasts app.

Voters are real, living and breathing human beings and citizens of their countries... so most importantly, digital liberals must talk to real people and love and embrace fellow neighbors as people. They cannot be judged by "Likes" or "usernames" hiding behind closed digital barriers.

4. Stop harping on identity politics – "racism," "bigotry," "xenophobia," etc.

Democrats own a monopoly of control in major American inner cities – all the "killing fields" like Chicago, Detroit, Baltimore, New Orleans and St. Louis. Democrats own these inner cities and have owned them for decades. Deep blue states run by liberal Democrats are going broke all over the United States. You can add Connecticut and socialist California to that list, per *Forbes* and *The Mercury News*. Democrats and progressives are largely responsible for much of what is wrong with the inner cities and many oppressions black people and other minorities suffer. Until now, lame Republicans have been too polite to notice this, but Trump has already made building up Black America a priority, calling for a "New Deal for Black America."

This will blow up the Democratic voting base and make digital liberals go haywire.

Digital liberals are sympathetic to our enemies abroad and domestic criminals at home – based on whether such folks are of a certain skin color.

Racial and identity politics will never be a winning strategy. Obama didn't use it in his campaigns, and he didn't use it against his opponents either.

Digital liberals are clueless that the last two Democratic presidents – Bill Clinton and Barack Obama – along with the entire Democratic Party leadership sold out their historic constituency: the working class.

Here's much of what killed the working class over the past 10 years:

- Wall Street deregulation
- Trillion-dollar bank bailouts after these institutions nearly destroyed the global economy and after committing fraud after fraud after fraud without anyone ever going to jail
- Letting homeowners go down the tubes with no bailouts, resulting in them losing their homes

-   A trillion-dollar giveaway to insurance companies and then allowing them to dictate our healthcare

If the Democrats and digital liberals don't understand this, which it appears they don't, then they shouldn't hold power at all. They aren't learning anything from their disastrous defeats. That's why they keep losing.

Despite Trump's low status with the mainstream media, Democrats still can't win. Their losses are mounting up in runoffs and in 2017 gubernatorial and mayoral races. They'll keep cheering "near-wins," but that's it.

Digital liberals focus too hard on identity politics, which only a tiny segment of the world gives a sh*t about.

When it comes to jobs or the economy, digital liberals have nothing. They shill for corporate America, which is transforming by the month because of the digitization of business and outsourcing.

The Left is against single-payer health care. They push "grand bargains" for Social Security, and they want open borders. They also support interventionist wars and regime changes.

The Democratic Party is also seen as corrupt. The Democratic establishment sabotaged Bernie Sanders in 2016. They saw Sanders as a threat because he wasn't a Democrat (he was Independent throughout his political career), exposed the corruption within the DNC, and went against their ideals — just like what the Republicans thought about Trump, but they swallowed their pride and got behind him for the good of their party. It's why Hillary and the Democrats didn't make Sanders the Vice Presidential nominee to counter Trump's populism. Clinton, the DNC and the media suppressed him. Clinton's running mate, Tim Kaine, barely even won them his blue state of Virginia — final count of about 49% to 45%. A Clinton/Sanders ticket would've smothered Trump's campaign and undecided voters to vote Democrat. Zero Hedge reports that many of Sanders' followers hated Hillary so much that they voted for Trump — or didn't vote at all.

To win, the Dems need to throw a true progressive into the fire...

Someone who doesn't advocate for longer prison sentences for minor crimes... someone who is against balanced budgets and fiscal conservatism... someone who's not in the pocket of big corporate donors.

Identity politics divided the Democrats and fringe voters in the Election of 2016, and it will be the downfall of the Democratic Party if it continues.

5. Stop giving Trump so much attention

You don't beat Trump by giving him more attention. You beat him by making him irrelevant. Do not love or hate him. Ignore him.

The solution is simple: if you want your person to win an election, then you publicize and promote your candidate only – for better or for worse.

Consider these examples from revisionist history...

Michael Moore shouldn't have been making movies about George W. Bush (*FAHRENHEIT 9/11* before the 2004 Election) and Trump (*TRUMPLAND* before the 2016 Election). He should have been making movies about John Kerry and Hillary Clinton if he wanted them to win.

Dinesh D'Souza shouldn't have been making a movie about President Barack Obama (*2016: OBAMA'S AMERICA* before the 2012 Election) if he wanted Obama to lose. He should've been making a movie about Mitt Romney.

Hillary Clinton made a huge mistake going after Trump in her advertisements instead of pumping herself up. She spent millions of dollars to tell the public not to vote for Trump and giving Trump more airtime instead of promoting herself and telling people to vote for her. That's a recipe for disaster because it shows cowardice and mistrust in oneself.

The converse applies to this principle too: If Hillary beat Trump during the 2016 Election, she would easily be re-elected in 2020... because the Right then would not shut up about her crookedness.

Chapter 21

WHY PRESIDENT DONALD TRUMP WILL BE REELECTED IN 2020

I believe in giving people a chance and seeing how things play out. I'm not succumbing to the media or fear-mongering. Three years from now, people on the fringe will look back and say, "Well, that wasn't so bad after all," and the digital liberals won't give up on their obsessions with anything "Trump."

Contrary to digital liberal opinion, the facts show that people should feel safer and optimistic about the future...

Innovation in this country is through the roof. The jobs are still in the U.S. *Reuters* reports that unemployment is at all-time lows this millennium. At one point well into Trump's Presidency, the U.S. dollar had been one of strongest of the millennium, and its status as the world reserve currency is going nowhere. The military is second to none. Murders and crimes in most urban cities outside the "killing fields" are way down this year compared to last year.

As of the publishing of this book in Q4 2017, Rasmussen – one of the most accurate polling sources of the 2016 Election along with The University of Southern California and Investor's Business Daily – has Trump at 52% approval.

Rasmussen also reported that President Donald Trump is MORE popular on this date of his presidency than Obama was.

This comes after months of the most biased, vicious, negative media coverage in modern history... where much of the mainstream media tried to destroy, slander, libel, excoriate, impeach, and convict Trump. This same media lied & committed fraud to make Obama a God... yet Trump is still MORE popular.

After firing the FBI Director...

After "obstruction of justice" accusations and investigations...

After nonstop damaging leaks of his conversations with world leaders...

After never-ending accusations of collusion and passing classified information to Russian leaders.

How can the Democrats compete in 2020? Their nominee will have to start from scratch. Trump has a head start of 63 million voters. Nobody of viable stature will want to compete with that.

You only get one chance at Presidency, which is why I don't think Michelle Obama or Cory Booker will run in 2020. They stand far better chances of winning a clean slate in 2024.

Hillary was the Democrats' best chance in 2016. Who will be their go-to in 2020?

Pocahontas (Elizabeth Warren) is the only viable candidate the Democrats have, and the digital liberals don't even know or care about her.

Gavin Newsom or Kamala Harris? Not qualified or experienced enough for establishment insiders...

Mark Cuban? He's a billionaire media personality just like Trump.

The Rock? *The People's Champ* knows how to give electrifying speeches and will have Hollywood backing him... just like Reagan in the early 80's.

But let's be serious here...

Donald Trump's party's record (which he has endorsed and is responsible for) is 5-0 in Special Elections since he won in November 2016.

5-0... as in undefeated. Perfect.

Therefore, I think Trump will be re-elected. The Democrats will not take control of the House of Representatives or Senate in 2018 because Trump has such a dogmatic following of people who'll do anything he tells them to do. The midterms won't even be competitive. All Trump needs to do is tell his people – with his usual Trumpian rhetoric – to go out and vote Republican. His people actually do and act on what he says.

It doesn't matter that Hurricane Maria has caused tens of thousands of Puerto Ricans to move to Florida. They will likely flip the state from red to blue, but it still won't be sufficient to win the general election.

Donald Trump's insanity has unified a large segment of people, but it's not enough to win back the country in 2020.

Digital liberals silenced a nation into quietly voting for Trump. As long as the Trump-shaming or alternative view-shaming continues, their behavior – evidenced through social media postings, violent or disturbing protests, solicitations of money (scamming) for recounts, and accusations of Russian hacking to sway elections – will only reinforce that this silent Electoral majority will vote for Trump again in 2020... and if the Dems place their leading candidate Elizabeth Warren in 2020, this will turn into the most lopsided Election of our lifetimes (Trump winning) – even greater than President Barack Obama's landslide in 2008 and Bill Clinton's in 1996.

Chapter 22

THE CRAZIEST TRUMP-RELATED FACEBOOK POSTS YOU'LL EVER SEE

In this chapter, I've pasted and responded to *funny / dumb / crazy/ thought-provoking / stupid Facebook posts* I came across pre and post-Election. These posts don't require long responses or their own chapters. This should be a quick and refreshing read-through.

Before the Election, I thought anti-Trumpers couldn't be more annoying on social media (as opposed to the silent pro-Trumpers and anti-Hillary campers, who were too afraid to speak up about anything pro-Trump or anti-Hillary).

Nearly one year later, I can say I was sorely mistaken...

They actually could get more annoying.

Beware: this could be the most entertaining part of the book.

"I've been crying nonstop since Tuesday night, and I can't help but feel confused, hurt, and betrayed by the people in this country."

"It is hard to wake up every morning. This grief is palpable and immense."

"I don't even have the words. I'm crying. I'm hurting. I have lost the hope, optimism, and general patriotism I felt for years leading up to this election."

"The past 48 hours have been so devastating. I couldn't stop myself from crying. It pains me to know that so many of the people I love, respect, who are different than me but are so so beautiful in those differences will be even more vulnerable than ever due to this nightmare that is reality."

My heart is hurting so much."

"I am truly sickened over all of this. My heart hurts and I just want to cry. Time to pray for strength, understanding and love. Good night and God help us please."

"Bawling my eyes out :-("

"I honestly am devastated and perhaps also due to lack of sleep i can't stop crying."

These are eight separate posts by eight different people. I've clumped them together because they capture the sentiment post-Election.

The Election of 2016 was a wakeup call to intolerant digital liberals. They got exactly what they deserved because they were delusional enough to not even see his victory coming. It's made nearly half the country laugh, smile and proud to see digital liberal tears about the very issues they created.

Those who profess to support tolerance and equality have become the most intolerant and chauvinistic.

The United States has too many emotionally weak people who feel vengeful about a corrupt, elitist, lying, self-serving, power-hungry, warmongering woman not being elected as the most powerful puppet in the world. #1stWorldProblems

Tens of millions of people didn't betray *you*. What makes YOU so important? You're an atom compared to the whole substance. If you walk outside and talk to some people with different viewpoints – they don't even have to be opposing – *you* just might learn something.

Not everyone can get their way all the time. If you expect to go through life by getting everything you want, then you'll eventually be diagnosed with depression. Crying a lot is one of the steps leading up to depression. The world will break your heart if you think it's going to treat you fairly or if you think your personal definition of "good" or "right" will prevail over "evil" or "wrong" all the time.

I hope all these people have been drinking lots of water.

People should not fear President Donald Trump. Humans have overcome much worse. We've made it this far. History tells us we will be fine.

"I drove off on my lunch break and cried in my car  *"*

If Trump winning the Election really meant something to you, then you'd be crying all day, every day... not just on your lunch break.

Did Republicans burn flags, cry a lot, and block traffic when Obama was elected twice?

No.

"This just in: California drought ended by liberal tears."

Who said Trump isn't an environmentalist? The man may not know the issues, but solutions come about because of him.

"Everybody at my school listen up. Desperate times call for desperate measures. Fuck class. Join hundreds of other students at a "Cry-in"... We need to just take a break and just cry. Tomorrow we get back up and keep fighting, because people feel really, really powerless."

FOX News reported that Cornell students shared their grief with a mass "cry-in" to mourn Trump's victory.

Professors at the University of Connecticut, University of Rochester and Iowa State University cancelled classes because they simply couldn't face the day.

College is a great time to grow up. The grief students face is a part of that process.

Students need to show gratitude to their loans or parents who are paying tuition. Skipping class because your "team lost" shows what a "Cup Cake Nation" we have become. These hypersensitive and overly emotional kids need to be toughened up – not offered "cry-ins" or "disaster counseling." We are educating a new generation of insecure wimps. If this is how teenagers and early 20-somethings will handle failure, then it will only be a matter of time until they join the new silent majority.

"I called my mom because quite frankly i needed mamas love, but she just gave me all kinds of hell and told me how dumb i was and wrong i was and not being godly and everything else she could say."

Momma knows best. Grow up and be a man. Momma shouldn't be raising you when you're above the age of 25.

"My friends here are all terrified. Im terrified. And so many people i love have let me know very clearly that they do not at all care."

We care about our own opinions more than other people's, yet we chase other people's approvals constantly.

You said your friends are all terrified. Then you said those you love "do not at all care."

What?

Enough said.

"These people are the worst monsters in modern history and you voted for them. You pieces of shit. I hate all of you right now."

Osama Bin Laden, Robert Mugabe, Omar al-Bashir, rapists, the Facebook Live murderer... Trump and Pence are worse than all of them!

"These people are pure evil and can't find it within their hearts to let others love (and pee) in peace!"

Incorrect... Trump loves those golden showers.

"Went through the 5 Stages of Grief in less than 36 hours. #JustKeepSwimming"

If I were this guy, I would've quickly written an e-book and come out with a course: "GOING THROUGH THE FIVE STAGES OF GRIEF IN LESS THAN 36 HOURS POST-ELECTION 2016." He would've made a quick buck.

"When I see you next I'll give you the biggest hug posible. When red hugs blue it's all purple stuff filed with love... but you were on my ballet and had my vote."

This male poster commented on a sentimental post that a female wrote. I like his pick-up ideas, but again, his execution (and spelling / grammar / punctuation) make him come across as desperate and illiterate.

"We are all heartbroken and disappointed and grieving. 51% nation just told us that we do not matter."

How the f*ck can, "51% of a nation" tell "us that we do not matter," yet, "We are all heartbroken and disappointed and grieving?" This poster should've instead said,"49% of us are..." not ALL of us.

Furthermore, why is this person assuming 51% of the nation knows who this poster is personally? Just because someone voted for a candidate doesn't mean they think people who didn't vote for that candidate don't matter... this logic is elementary.

In other words, just because you vote for someone doesn't mean you are that person or agree with everything they say...

"What am I supposed to tell my kids in the morning? I can only pray for their futures and protect them the best I can."

Easy... tell your kids, "Donald Trump is our new President." End of discussion...

Kids don't get together to talk politics around the water cooler.

They drink Mountain Dew and play video games.

When I was a kid and heard people talking politics, I got bored.

When I was a teenager and heard people talking politics, I got bored.

Politics is boring. You don't see a bunch of babies watching CNN or FOX News.

I didn't REALLY start following politics until two years ago, and that was only because Trump sucked me in. I was in my mid-20's at the time.

I was 9 when the Bill Clinton sex scandal happened. I didn't even know what sex was. My parents' response to me when I asked them what the President and news were talking about went something like, "Somebody saw the President kissing a girl on the cheek at the White House. He is apologizing to his wife and now she is getting ready to divorce him, so he's saying things to keep his wife from leaving."

It wasn't until a few years ago – nearly 20 years later – that I found out about the truth, including the cigar. If you don't know what I'm talking about, just Google, "Bill Clinton Monica Lewinsky cigar."

I'd say I've done well for myself despite not knowing anything about politics or political scandals.

You can too.

"Trump and his millions of supporters have everyone in this country upset."

How can "everyone" be upset at Trump if 49% of voters in this country support him? If "everyone" is upset with him, shouldn't he have no supporters?

"I couldn't sleep last night and I can't stop crying. I am heartbroken. I want to blame so many people for what happened last night. I pray for safety."

Blame half the country... each and every single one of those people who showed up to the polls and voted Trump. They outnumber you, your circle, and your ideas.

"How is one supposed to grieve when you have to be at work?"

Nobody is making "one" or "you" be at work. If grieving at home is more important, then call in sick... and learn some pronoun agreement while you're at it.

"America = trash"

I actually like this post. It's short and sweet, with very little dumb thought behind it.

"How is it even possible that there are so many people stupid enough to vote?"

I guess you're smart and nearly half the nation is stupid. This is a good thing! There is no excuse for you to struggle academically, professionally or financially. Less competition... you should celebrate!!!

"There has never been a time where the market went down this fast within hours."

Look up the Flash Crash. The DOW crashed nearly 900 points in less than five minutes.

In addition, the market finished up the day Trump was elected (he was officially elected in the early morning of November 9, 2016).

"No country will ever take us serious again."

It's hard to take posters *seriously* when they don't know English grammar.

The United States has the largest military in the world. Nobody can come remotely close to competing with it — not even Russia or all the terrorist groups combined. Other countries have everything to fear when it comes to going against the United States.

Furthermore, the U.S. economy takes up more than half of the world economy. The country with the next largest economy is China at approximately 20%... so two Chinas still wouldn't come close to the economic superpower that is the United States.

What does this mean? It means a country *has* to do business with the U.S. if it wants to globalize and reach new economic heights. The U.S. has money... and the customers.

"I'm scared for all of us here and our jobs. Our health and our future. Our safety especially when it comes to climate change and for us women, the issue of rape will never be properly prosecuted again under Trump. We all might as well take preventative birth control so we dont get pregnant with a rapist baby that pence will keep us from aborting. It sounds harsh, but its gonna be true. We are gonna turn into a 3rd world nation. We will lose our electricity. I know i dont want to live like this. Im praying ebola comes back and finds me so i dont have to live through these tough times."

Wow, this one wins... enough said.

"Trump is going to deport American citizens. He has no respect for our country or our military. He is going to take away women's rights to vote. If you're not beautiful, he'll send you to the kitchen to make corn bread."

No comment...

Actually, one comment...

Critics say Trump is against women, but a woman – Kellyanne Conway – ran his campaign and led him to victory. No woman had ever managed a successful Presidential campaign before... until the 2016 Election – thanks to Trump.

"All Trump cares about is fucking people over just so people on top can money while we all go without drinking water, crops and fields being destroyed and sacred land being disrespected."

I'm sure this is "all Trump cares about" and what he thinks about all day and in his sleep.

"The sun rises and sets and we move forward, albeit more determined than ever to be the best versions of ourselves that we can be. All we can do is keep breathing."

Yes.

"SHOCK - We called President-Elect Donald J. Trump's cell phone at 8:28am. He answered, agreed to go on the air with me. My level of shock may have outweighed my ability to do a good job."

I want this chapter to be insightful and informative too – not just funny or douchey.

This was posted by a former broadcast journalism classmate of mine at Syracuse University's S.I. Newhouse School of Public Communications. He is now a reporter / anchor / producer.

"The Muslim woman taking my order at Starbucks could tell I was emotionally-drained and she smiled at me."

Yes, I'm sure a complete stranger who works at Starbucks could tell you were emotionally drained. I'm also sure that she smiled at you and you only during her work shift as a barista.

"Ladies: if you don't already have one, I would strongly encourage you to consider getting an IUD before Trump takes office, in case the Affordable Care Act is repealed and birth control no longer covered by insurance. I have one and would be happy to answer any questions about it."

Whatever I say about this post will get me into trouble... so I won't say anything.

"I want to leave the USA soon but can't because my whole life and family are here."

Let me get this straight...

You loved the United States so much that you invested and built your entire life in it... and now, because your candidate didn't win, you want to leave?

If you're mad about one person out of the hundreds of millions of people who live here, then become emotionally tougher.

Get out if you don't like the U.S. Take your family and life with you. If you hate it so much, then you'll be better off elsewhere.

"Donald J. Trump is set for many trials, one of which is in December for raping a 14 year old girl."

This poster fell victim to the fake news pandemic.

Fake news isn't just started by fake news agencies and publishers. People make up their own sh*t on social media too.

We now live in a society where fake news outperforms real news. A *BuzzFeed News* analysis found that top fake election news stories generated more total engagement on Facebook than top election stories from 19 major news outlets combined.

"I have unfriended my annoying drunk uncle in San Antonio. I know that sounds terrible with family, but I don't feel bad about it at all. He deserves it for what he said to me here and in private messages."

Very sad that families have been torn apart because of their close-mindedness... both digital liberals and digital conservatives are to blame for this.

"Dear White People,

It is time to get YOUR people. So many of my White friends have access to their White family members and White friends who voted for Trump. We (PEOPLE OF COLOR & marginalized groups) NEED you to take responsibility for YOUR people. I don't need you to tell me how ashamed you are of your family and friends. WE need you to talk to them, we need you to confront them, we need you to be the bridge. If you are not willing to have the difficult conversations with your people don't say you stand with us against oppression and White supremacy.

Sincerely,

Angry Black Woman"

This "Angry Black Woman" has some serious self-esteem issues and needs a therapist. The fact that she's calling out, "Dear White People," on Facebook shows that she has no white friends. I knew her from college, and she refused to mingle with anyone who wasn't black. And now she's angry?

Please.

"There are racist trump supporters. Don't be pretending like they don't exist. Millions of people want to make America great again meaning back to a time where Jim Crow was the law of the land."

WTF? Most Americans don't even know what Jim Crow was. People be crazy.

I could easily say whoever voted for Hillary believes in colluding with Wall Street, media (evidenced by the removal of Debbie Wasserman Schultz as Chair of the DNC), corporatists (look at her donations), and terrorist nations (Clinton Foundation donations to countries funding terrorism and her incompetence as Secretary of State), which would make them crooks and terrorists themselves.

They would also believe in using their spouses for political gains despite the spouse's repeated affairs and sexual assault accusations. Therefore, they believe in sexual assault and are sexual assaulters.

Oh yeah, and Hillary stuck with her top aide Huma Abedin, who was going to be her Chief of Staff. The Hill reports that Abedin's family has ties to the Muslim Brotherhood, and her husband is under investigation for child pedophilia. So, because Hillary supports such a woman, that means her voters support child pedophilia too.

But I would never use such logic in arguments or as defenses because they are baseless conjectures of illogical thoughts.

Just because people vote for Trump doesn't mean they're racist or want to go back to Jim Crow. People have reasons to vote outside of racism.

There just aren't enough racists to make enough of a political difference on a national scale. If there were, then Obama would've never become President. He wouldn't have even made it past the primaries... and George Wallace and KKK Imperial Wizard David Duke would've been elected in the past.

There are people who voted twice for Obama in 2008 and 2012 yet voted for Trump in 2016. Racism cannot be the reason for this. Such people are not racist.

There are also white supremacist racists who voted against Obama – nearly 100% – twice in 2008 and 2012 because of his half black skin color. The results show that their votes didn't matter, for Obama still won in landslides.

What does this all mean?

Again, there just aren't enough racist white supremacists to swing an Election.

But this poster is absolutely correct... there are racist Trump supporters. There's no denying racist Trump supporters like there's no denying that there were racist Gary Johnson and Hillary Clinton supporters.

After all, no family has incarcerated more blacks than the Clintons. That's quite a feat considering the Kennedys were around pre-civil rights and for a much longer time. The Daily Beast reported that the Clintons have incarcerated more blacks than any other family this country has witnessed. There's only been two of them who've been around for four decades post-Civil Rights. The Kennedys, on the other hand, have been around far longer with a lot more people pre-Civil Rights... and the Clintons have still persecuted more blacks.

"I signed a bill that made the problem worse," Hillary Clinton said about black incarceration in July 2016.

Bill and Hillary have been true masters of deception. They can say whatever they want, but that's a horrible history of race relations based on what they've done.

"You should acknowledge our hurt and offer solace. If you know any Trump supporters who aren't racist, please introduce us to them."

You should get your eyes checked first — just to make sure they're working. I'm no doctor, but it seems you have a case of blindness.

You obviously have few friends unlike you. Again, there's a good chance one out of two people you stop on the street have no issues with Trump.

Sadly, as evidenced by digital liberal closed-mindedness and vitriolic language today, they are not willing to change or accept the other side.

Trump supporters are everywhere. One out of two people in this country support him. They're just in the closet because people like this poster silence and shame them.

This is not a good sign for 2020. If this continues, then Trump will have no problem being re-elected... and the Republicans will have no problem finding a candidate (like Mike Pence) to fill his shoes in 2024.

I know countless Trump voters who aren't racist and would be glad to introduce you to them. They are great people who have changed many lives, including mine. The CEOs of more than half my clients support him (many of whom are minorities). My financial planner voted for him. I hang out or talk to Trump supporters every day. They are a part of nearly half of the country supporting him. These are tech executives, Wall Street traders, entrepreneurs, blacks, Indians, Muslims, etc.

I also work with and hang out with people who support Democrats, Socialists, Libertarians, Communists too.

"I was on some super petty shit pre and post election. I unfriended anyone who voted for Donald, had a Donald in their name, was married to a Donald, or was related to a Donald."

"Did any of my friends vote for Donald Trump? If you have, please let me know so I can remove you from my Facebook friends list. I do not want to know you, talk to you, or deal with you ever again. You are dead to me. If you don't admit it, you can either

unfriend me and go away like the coward you are, or you can have me hunt you down so I can end our friendship."

This is the digital liberal bullsh*t that just gives the conservatives and even moderates more ammunition. Of all people, this second post was written by a doctor. It makes sense that he's not an M.D. and wasn't smart enough to be medically educated in the U.S. despite growing up here.

This guy doesn't understand that real, breathing people showed up to the polls in November 2016 to elect Donald Trump into office. A small subset of the population did not do this. If so, Trump wouldn't have won.

What does this mean to this poster? Patients whom he meets and treats every day voted for Trump. Just because they voted for him does not mean they are bad people or that they deserve to go untreated.

Social media comes with a lot of pitfalls, and one of those is that people have to watch what they say. There are a lot of digital liberals out there with love in their hearts who will wish you dead if they suspect you voted for Donald Trump.

"I am being very, very genuine when I say I would love to set up a Skype session to speak to esteemed professionals who voted for Trump. To be honest, I have yet to cross a Trump supporter who I can have an enlightening conversation with."

This is what is so shocking... not a knock directly on this poster, but for all critics of democracy.

All this poster needs to do is go to Donald Trump's Facebook Fan Page and see all her friends who "Like" it. When I did this, I saw hundreds of my friends.

Too much of this country lives in their own bubble and refuses to acknowledge other sides or opinions once they've made up their mind on surface issues.

You have to consider: Trump got THE MOST ELECTORAL VOTES OF ANY REPUBLICAN NOMINEE since 1988, and he got THE MOST POPULAR VOTES OF ANY REPUBLICAN NOMINEE EVER. That's a lot of people who VOTED for him. There aren't enough racists or white supremacists to cover this number.

There are people who voted twice for Obama in 2008 and 2012 yet voted for Trump in 2016. Racism cannot be the reason for this. Such people are not racist.

There are also white supremacist racists who voted against Obama – nearly 100% – twice in 2008 and 2012 because of his half black skin color. The results show that their votes didn't matter, for Obama still won in landslides.

What does this all mean?

Again, there just aren't enough racist white supremacists to swing an Election.

There are Trump supporters who are uneducated racist hillbillies. That's a fact...

But there are countless supporters who are not...

They like his strategy to defeat ISIS. They like low taxes. They want the borders protected. They like that he's anti-establishment and a disruption to the status quo and political elite.

This movement was not tiny. More people voted in the 2016 Election than in any other Election ever before.

There are too many opinions out there and not enough realism or acceptance of 21st century trends and affairs.

"The American people desire a leader who represents American values."

One person did not make the decision for Trump to be President. An entire nation of people voted, and he came out victorious. These people "desired" for him to be their leader.

While Trump may have some negative values (we all do), the voters decided that he better represents their American values more than his competition.

"It won't be so funny when Cheeto head has to explain to America why he ruined the stock market and the world economy overnight. Hope you are happy."

The stock market went on an insane bull run post-Election.

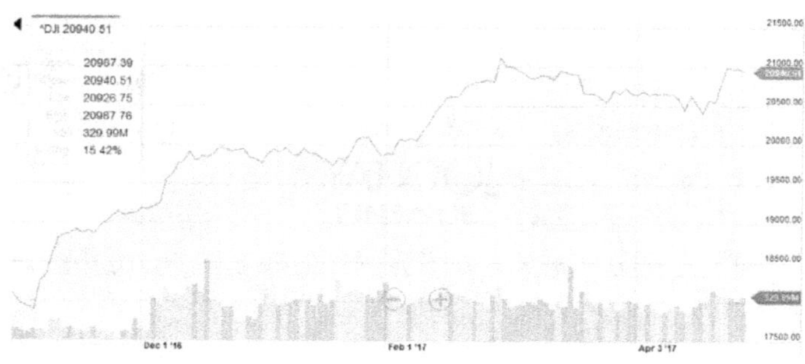

I am truly afraid for my beard.

Shave it off. You'll get more girls.

"Liberalism in America finally died today and socialism is the only answer moving forward."

This person has no clue what socialism is. When has socialism been the answer to building a strong economy? Fighting — and winning — successful wars? Human rights? Gay / transgender rights? Private property rights? Lower taxes?

"Presidents should have the ability to sell decisions to ALL the people in their country, not just a subset."

This is impossible in a capitalist, democratic republic.

Obama's lack of attention to the country isolated tens of millions of people who enabled Trump to get elected in the first place.

It's impossible to make everyone happy.

"Trump should make decisions that a majority of people want... not his minority of supporters."

A majority of the House of Representatives and a majority of Senate support Donald Trump's moves. A majority of the Electoral College supports him too.

Real, breathing people showed up to the polls in November to elect Trump into office. A small subset of the population did not do this. If so, he wouldn't have won.

The U.S. democratic system is the Electoral College. Had it been a popular vote system, then the rules and strategies would've been completely different. The Washington Post reports that Trump could have beaten Hillary Clinton in a popular vote as well. It would have simply been a different campaign approach and strategy.

I wonder how many World Series championships have been stolen from the team who scored the most runs throughout the series. NBA Finals too... in 2013, the San Antonio Spurs scored more points than the Miami Heat – 684-679 – but the Heat won the series 4-3 (four games to three), and the NBA Championship. #NotFair

I'm starting to like Trump he might be a clown but he gangsta AF. He said good luck bringing me down Ima just fire ya ass These fools in Capitol Hill ain't ready for a gangsta too take over lol

"If u can't beat them, fuck it join them. Make America Great Again..."

This made me laugh... always a good strategy.

"WOW!!! This Debate is Clearly rigged as Trump is not even allowed to respond to that stupid Cunt! She can talk all her shit about him and then they cut him off when he responds? total BULLSHIT!!!! Im so sick of this one sided bullshit!!!! I hope Hillary fucking Dies!!!!! and If you don't like what I have to say, you know where the Unfriend Button is.. please feel free to use it!!!"

I don't want this to become a pro-Trump book. Rather, it's a book that addresses the misinformation surrounding President Trump.

There are Trump supporters who are emotional idiots too. This poster is one of them.

Although I personally enjoy reading enthusiastic hate like "*!!!!*" instead of dramatic sh*t like "☹" or ":'-(".

STAY IN TOUCH

Tweet me @xnareshx.

Visit www.nareshvissa.com to subscribe to my FREE newsletter mailing list.

If you have any questions or would like to get in touch, e-mail me at naresh at krishmediamarketing dot com.

For a full list of services my full-service online business solutions agency Krish Media & Marketing offers, visit www.krishmediamarketing.com.

Please leave a review of this book on Amazon!

AFTERWORD

By Gerald Celente

Founder of the Trends Research Institute
Publisher of the Trends Journal
www.TrendsResearch.com

There was no better-suited stage to reflect just how deep America's collective smarts, dignity, self-pride and morality had sunk than Presidential Campaign 2016.

Today, two-thirds of Americans are asking themselves how the hell we elected Donald Trump president. How did so many supposedly level-headed, moderate voters in Rust Belt states and elsewhere place their votes — and hopes for real, dynamic change — in the lap of Trump?

Look in the mirror, America.

The Shadow Knows

Perhaps in the deep recesses of what is known as depth psychology we find some answers, a larger context, for understanding America's decline and the rise of the Presidential Reality Show.

The concept of the Shadow, created by the great Swiss psychologist Carl Jung, provides insights into an America struggling to think for itself.

In particular, for digital liberals – as Naresh Vissa calls them in this book – Trump has become their Shadow.

The Shadow is an unconscious component of our personalities that stores the ugly, dark stuff we can't face in waking reality. As individuals, groups of people, organizations, countries and, of course, political parties reject facing the ugly, hard truth staring them in the face long enough, the more powerful and destructive their Shadow becomes.

Eventually, you display your failure to accept the truth. You become uncharacteristically angry, emotional, illogical and uncentered.

Under President Barack Obama, liberal Democrats stood silent and numb for eight years.

Where were they when, under Obama's watch, 95 percent of wealth gained in the US went to the 1 percent, and 51 percent of full-time workers earned less than $30,000 a year?

Where was the Left when anti-war fraud, Nobel Peace of crap prize-winner Obama bragged about his 30,000-troop surge into Afghanistan? Silent when he said, "I'm really good at killing people," referring to his drone strikes that killed over 4,000 innocent people and fueled Muslim hatred toward America. Where were those peace-loving, anti-war mongers when Obama ordered bombing campaigns that continued to fuel Muslim hatred in seven countries?

What about stealing our rights through the National Security Agency and the famous Patriot Act, robbing us of our *habeas corpus*, that Obama signed into law in 2011 on New Year's Eve when no one was paying attention?

Where was the Left? Hiding in the Shadow. What it has denied and repressed about itself, it now projects on Trump, the Right and any other entity or person reflecting a contradictory viewpoint.

Denial, Denial, Denial

During the Obama years, liberals lost their morality, integrity, passion, purpose and drive. They rejected facts and realities before them, relegating them to storage bin of denials Jung called the Shadow. And when Obama's tenure was over, the Shadow was cast across the country, especially among liberals and moderates.

The *Trends Journal* was the first magazine (Spring 2016 edition) to predict Trump would win and why. And when he did win, we wrote:

"Handing the Obama legacy off to Hillary Clinton signaled to the American populace 'more of the same.' In contrast, Trump's simple message — It's about the economy, stupid — resonated" (*Trends Journal*, Fall 2016).

Now, the nation is more divided than ever. And the so-called Left, smoldering in its state of shock, only rallies against narcissism, racism, sexism, Nazism and anti-Semitism under a new party label, "The Resistance," but remains anti-war silent.

Resistance is more denial.

"We cannot change anything until we accept it," Jung said. "Condemnation does not liberate; it oppresses.

For eight years under Obama, liberals denied, ignored and sat quiet while hypocrisy reigned over their party. They set the stage for a Trump-like figure, who used simple messaging and unorthodox tactics not only to win, but send much of the country into a tailspin, seeking answers and unifying opposition.

Under the guise of exceptionalism, that holier-than-thou mindset that feeds more denial and more deposits into the Shadow's unconscious, America and especially those who call themselves liberal created the flipside of the Great American Dream.

We're living and dying in Dumfuckistan.

Declining State of Liberalism

Throughout 2017, anti-Donald Trump graffiti has spread across Colonial Kingston, New York, defacing artifacts, landmarks and public properties where the seeds of democracy were sown.

In front of the circa 1700 Dr. Jansen house, its historic stone Carriage Step has been damaged by indelible black ink with the graffiti, "Corrupt. Expensive, Useless. This is our President. Now, traitorous to?"

At this historic intersection and throughout Colonial Kingston, bluestone sidewalks and buildings have been desecrated with anti-Trump graffiti such as "Trump equals poison," and those supporting him "can neither see nor smell the stinking swamp he is!"

I acquired three of these richly historic buildings not only to restore and preserve them as tribute to Kingston's vital role in the birth of the nation, but also as an act of patriotism. I am outraged that some disrespectful hypocrite who attacks Trump as being "poison" and "vulgar" takes it upon himself or herself to desecrate this historic community with poisonous graffiti.

This has nothing to do with politics – who you like or who you hate. It's about the reckless disregard for the city – its people, traditions and treasures.

Day by day, the anti-Trump graffiti continues to spread throughout this historic area. To have some thoughtless lowlife etch his or her anger on the very foundation of American history is a pathetic commentary on the state of liberals.

The Obama years ended with him vigorously campaigning for Hillary Clinton in her race against Donald Trump. No president in history campaigned harder for his potential successor than Obama did, pleading with voters to support Clinton and, thus, endorse his legacy.

His campaigning capped off the stunning failure of war-hawk and pseudo-liberal Clinton to generate enough enthusiasm to beat what the polls say was the weakest presidential candidate in history. The result? What was left of the Left was annihilated.

Liberals, Progressives and Leftists... these are antiquated, meaningless labels of what they once symbolized. With high voter disgust for Democrats, as exemplified by not only by the presidential election, but massive election losses on federal and state House levels, and high distrust among the huge millennial generation who believe the nomination of their candidate, Bernie Sanders, was stolen by Democratic Party leaders, the progressive movement and its so-called liberal media have no focus, energy, purpose or passion.

The fish rots from the head down. And the Left, which professes "progressive" values such as being anti-war, anti-big brother and anti-big corporation but remained silent when Obama launched wars, expanded government surveillance, pushed for global trade and let

Wall Street banksters go free, helped build the stage for the coming of Trump.

There's a phrase in Jungian circles that the Left should heed:

It's time they "eat their shadow."

Gerald Celente
Founder of the Trends Research Institute
Publisher of the Trends Journal
www.TrendsResearch.com

REFERENCES

"1. The American Family Today." *Pew Research Center's Social & Demographic Trends Project*. N.p., 17 Dec. 2015. Web.

Abrams, Hannah. "Colin Kaepernick in Trouble Over Fidel Castro T-Shirt." *Promo Marketing*, 30 Nov. 2016, magazine.promomarketing.com/article/colin-kaepernick-trouble-fidel-castro-t-shirt/.

"Actors and Photographers Wanted in Charlotte." *Craigslist*. N.p., n.d. Web.

Alarkon, Walter, and Kevin Bogardus. "Lawmakers Frustrated over Obama Plan to Cut Funds for Black Colleges." *TheHill*. N.p., 04 Feb. 2016. Web.

"American Civil War Ends." *History.com*, A&E Television Networks, www.history.com/this-day-in-history/american-civil-war-ends.

Asher, Jeff. "U.S. Cities Experienced Another Big Rise In Murder In 2016." *FiveThirtyEight*. FiveThirtyEight, 09 Jan. 2017. Web.

Associated Press. "Spurs Fined $250,000 for 'disservice'." *ESPN*. ESPN Internet Ventures, 01 Dec. 2012. Web.

Beckett, Lois, Aliza Aufrichtig, and Kenan Davis. "Murders up 10.8% in Biggest Percentage Increase since 1971, FBI Data Shows." *The Guardian*. Guardian News and Media, 26 Sept. 2016. Web.

Benjamin, Medea. "America Dropped 26,171 Bombs in 2016. What a Bloody End to Obama's Reign | Medea Benjamin." *The Guardian*. Guardian News and Media, 09 Jan. 2017. Web.

"Bill Clinton Being Asked About "THE CIGAR" By Special Prosecutor." *YouTube*. YouTube, 12 Aug. 2016. Web.

Blake, Aaron. "Donald Trump Says He Would Have Won a Popular-vote Election. And He Could Be Right." *The Washington Post*. WP Company, 15 Nov. 2016. Web.

Bodenner, Chris. "The Racist Legacy of Woodrow Wilson, Cont'd." *The Atlantic*. Atlantic Media Company, 30 Nov. 2015. Web.

Bradlee, Benjamin C. *That Special Grace*. N.p.: Lippincott, 1964. Print.

Brown, Travis H. "Hartford, Hit with Brunt of Connecticut Tax Hike, Hires Bankruptcy Attorney." *Forbes*. Forbes Magazine, 10 July 2017. Web.

Butler, Erika. "Bel Air Police Detain Woman Walking, Question Her Immigration Status." *The Aegis*. N.p., 27 Jan. 2017. Web.

Byrnes, Jesse. "Clinton: 'I Signed a Bill That Made the Problem Worse, and I Want to Admit It'." *TheHill*. N.p., 01 Feb. 2016. Web.

Campbell, Stephen. "2020 United States Presidential Odds." *Odds Shark*. OddsShark, 21 May 2017. Web.

CBS/AP. "University of Tampa Fires Professor Who Blamed Harvey on GOP Vote." *CBS News*, CBS Interactive, 29 Aug. 2017, www.cbsnews.com/news/kenneth-storey-university-of-tampa-fires-professor-who-blamed-harvey-on-gop-vote/.

Cooper, Jonathan J. "$1.9 Billion Error Adds to California Deficit Projection." *The Mercury News.* The Mercury News, 19 Jan. 2017. Web.

Corosaniti, Nick. "Donald Trump Gets Cool Reception at Black Church in Flint, Mich." *The New York Times.* The New York Times, 14 Sept. 2016. Web.

"Crowds on Demand." *Crowds on Demand.* N.p., n.d. Web.

Daugherty, Alex. "The Trump Whisperer: Marco Rubio Has the President's Ear on Latin America." *Miamiherald.* N.p., 26 June 2017. Web.

"Donald Trump Access Hollywood UNCENSORED." *YouTube.* YouTube, 07 Oct. 2016. Web.

Durden, Tyler. ""I'm A Bernie Sanders Voter.. Here's Why I'll Vote Trump"." *ZeroHedge.* N.p., 2 Oct. 2016. Web.

Durden, Tyler. "Journalists Drink Too Much, Are Dumber Than Average, Study Finds." *ZeroHedge.* N.p., 18 May 2017. Web.

Durden, Tyler. "The Real Lesson For America As Grubhub Stock Plunges After CEO Tells Trump Supporters To Resign." *ZeroHedge.* N.p., 11 Nov. 2016. Web.

"Emancipation Proclamation." *Wikipedia*, Wikimedia Foundation, 27 Aug. 2017, en.wikipedia.org/wiki/Emancipation_Proclamation.

FactPointVideo. "Two New Anti-Trump Attack Ads Launched by Hillary Clinton." *YouTube.* YouTube, 04 May 2016. Web.

"FLASHBACK: 2011: Obama Paused Iraq Refugee Program for Six Months." *Fox News.* FOX News Network, 30 Jan. 2017. Web.

Frank, T.A. "The Alleged Trump-Putin." *The Hive.* Vanity Fair, 25 May 2017. Web.

Fingerhut, Hannah. "4. Top Voting Issues in 2016 Election." *Pew Research Center for the People and the Press*, 7 July 2016, www.people-press.org/2016/07/07/4-top-voting-issues-in-2016-election/.

Gilmore, Scott. "Canada's Racism Problem? It's Even Worse than America's." *Macleans.ca*, 16 Mar. 2017, www.macleans.ca/news/canada/out-of-sight-out-of-mind-2/.

Gockowski, Anthony. "Profs Cancel Classes to 'cope' with 'anxiety and Terror' of Trump Win." *Campus Reform*. N.p., 09 Nov. 2016. Web.

Graaf, Mia De. "Neighbors of Husband and Wife San Bernardino Shooters 'noticed Them Acting Suspiciously but Did NOT Report Them for Fear of Racial Profiling'." *Daily Mail Online*. Associated Newspapers, 04 Dec. 2015. Web.

Grinberg, Emanuella. "Confederate Monument in Tampa Will Stay Put." *CNN*. Cable News Network, 22 June 2017. Web.

"The Hartman Media Company by Jason Hartman." *Hartman Media*, hartmanmedia.com/.

Haynes, Chris. "Stephen Curry Explains Why He's Locked in but Logged off." *ESPN*. ESPN Internet Ventures, 19 Apr. 2017. Web.

Henry, Zoë. "The Brilliant Business Model Behind Kim Kardashian's $150 Million App." *Inc.com*. Inc., 2 June 2015. Web.

"High School Dropout Rate on the Rise." *NBCNews.com*. NBCUniversal News Group, n.d. Web.

Holiday, Ryan. *Trust Me, I'm Lying: The Tactics and Confessions of a Media Manipulator*. N.p.: Portfolio/Penguin, 2013. Print.

Huddleston, Jr. Tom. "The Trump-Clinton Debate Could Get Super Bowl-Sized Ratings." *Trump Clinton Presidential Debate Could Get Super Bowl-Sized Ratings | Fortune.com*. Fortune, 26 Sept. 2016. Web.

Ibankcoin. "CNN EXPOSED IN UNDERCOVER STING! Producer Says Trump - Russia Story Fake News!" *YouTube*. YouTube, 26 June 2017. Web.

"Incarceration Rate for African-Americans Now Six times the National Average." *RT International*. N.p., n.d. Web.

"Indian Americans Voted for Trump in Significant Numbers." *The Hindu*. N.p., 11 Nov. 2016. Web.

"India–United States Civil Nuclear Agreement." *Wikipedia*. Wikimedia Foundation, 19 Aug. 2017. Web.

"Is Japan Really Racist?" *Japan Today*. N.p., 11 Nov. 2013. Web.

Join Together Staff. "New Data Show Millions of Americans with Alcohol and Drug Addiction Could Benefit from Health Care Reform." *Partnership for Drug-Free Kids - Where Families Find Answers*. N.p., n.d. 28 September. 2010. Web.

Kasperkevic, Jana, and Heidi Moore. "Anatomy of a Hoax: How a 17-year-old Built a Crazy Rumour That Swept Financial Media." *The Guardian*. Guardian News and Media, 20 Dec. 2014. Web.

"King of Vegas." *Wikipedia*, Wikimedia Foundation, 20 July 2017, en.wikipedia.org/wiki/King_of_Vegas.

King, Shaun. "KING: Thomas Jefferson Was an Evil Rapist Who Owned 600 Slaves." *NY Daily News.* N.p., 07 July 2017. Web.

Kipling, Rudyard. "If-." *Poetry Foundation.* Poetry Foundation, n.d. Web.

Kolodner, Meredith. "Even When Graduation Rates Rise, Black Students at Many Colleges Get Left behind." *The Hechinger Report.* N.p., 22 Mar. 2016. Web.

"Krish Media & Marketing." *Krish Media & Marketing.* N.p., n.d. Web.

Laila, Cristina. "Debbie Wasserman Schultz 'Absolute Wreck — Barely Able to Function' Since Imran Awan Arrest." *The Gateway Pundit.* N.p., 28 July 2017. Web.

Lederman, Doug. "Graduated but Not Literate." *Inside Higher Ed.* N.p., n.d. Web.

Lee, Dawn. "Single Mother Statistics." *Single Mother Guide.* N.p., 22 Aug. 2017. Web.

Levine, Daniel S. "Over 90 Million Eligible Voters Didn't Vote in the 2016 Presidential Election." *Heavy.com*. N.p., 10 Jan. 2017. Web.

LilWayneVEVO. "Lil Wayne - Rich As Fuck (Explicit) Ft. 2 Chainz." *YouTube*. YouTube, 23 Mar. 2013. Web.

Llenas, Bryan. "Boss Says Employees Who Agree with Trump's Rhetoric Should Resign." *Fox News*. FOX News Network, 10 Nov. 2016. Web.

MarkDice. "Meryl Streep Cries Over Donald Trump at Golden Globes." *YouTube*. YouTube, 08 Jan. 2017. Web.

McRady, Rachel. "Kanye West Tells Concertgoers He Would Have Voted for Donald Trump, Talks His 2020 Campaign." *Yahoo! Music*. Yahoo!, 18 Nov. 2016. Web.

"Media Entrepreneur, Author, Online Marketing Consultant & Sales Strategist." *Naresh Vissa*. N.p., n.d. Web.

Miller, Candice S. "H.R.158 - Visa Waiver Program Improvement and Terrorist Travel Prevention

Act of 2015." *Congress.gov.* N.p., 9 Dec. 2015. Web.

Moore, Antonio. "African-Americans Didn't Do Well Under President Obama." *Newsmax.* Newsmax Inc. Newsmax Inc., 21 Dec. 2016. Web.

Moore, Matt. "Everyone's Out: Warriors to Rest Steph Curry, Thompson, Green against Spurs." *CBSSports.com.* N.p., 11 Mar. 2017. Web.

Moraes, Lisa De. "CNN Scores Best Debate Ratings In Its History As Fox News Fans Face Vs Debate 1 In Wake Of Donald Trump Lewd Remarks." *Deadline.* N.p., 10 Oct. 2016. Web.

Moreno, Amy. "BREAKING : The Past SIX Presidents Have "Banned Immigrants"." *TruthFeed.* TruthFeed, 29 Jan. 2017. Web.

Morin, Rich. "America's Four Middle Classes." *Pew Research Center's Social & Demographic Trends Project,* 28 July 2008, www.pewsocialtrends.org/2008/07/29/america s-four-middle-classes/.

Mullen, Rodger. "Lara Trump Delivers Groceries in Fayetteville for Flood Victims." *The Fayetteville Observer.* The Fayetteville Observer, 13 Oct. 2016. Web.

Mutikani, Lucia. "U.S. Job Growth Slows; Unemployment Rate Drops to 4.3 Percent." *Reuters.* Thomson Reuters, 02 June 2017. Web.

"Narrative Pt. III: Continued Sexual Encounters." *The Washington Post.* WP Company, 1998. Web.

"National Tracking Poll." *Morning Consult.* N.p., n.d. Web.

nesn-staff on Sun, Jan 20, 2013 at 7:57PM. "Colin Kaepernick Still Owns Now-115-Pound Tortoise He Got When He Was 10 Years Old (Photo)." *NESN.com,* 21 Jan. 2013, nesn.com/2013/01/colin-kaepernick-still-owns-a-now-115-pound-tortoise-he-got-when-he-was-10-photo/.

"NewsPro Ranks Newhouse Top Journalism School in Nation." *The Daily Orange — The Independent Student Newspaper of Syracuse, New York.* N.p., n.d. Web.

Nicholas, Peter, and Daniel Lippman. "Wall Street Is Still Giving to President." *The Wall Street Journal.* Dow Jones & Company, 03 July 2012. Web.

Norton, Ben. "U.S. Acknowledges Israel's Unlawful Killings, Excessive Force, Torture, Discrimination Against..." *Salon.* N.p., 19 Apr. 2016. Web.

O'Connell, Michael. "Jeff Zucker Talks Trump TV and CNN's Ratings Hot Streak: We've "Outshined Everybody"." *The Hollywood Reporter.* N.p., 27 Oct. 2016. Web.

"Omarosa Manigault." *Wikipedia.* Wikimedia Foundation, 22 Aug. 2017. Web.

O'Neill, Kara. "This Video of Men 'injecting Dogs with Acid Has Sparked Outrage." *Mirror.* N.p., 22 Apr. 2015. Web.

Perabo, Lyonel. "Is Barack Obama Underestimated in America in Terms of Domestic Affairs and Policy on the International Stage? Why?" *Quora.* N.p., 5 Mar. 2016. Web.

Perry, Simon, and Michael Miller. "George Clooney Blasts Donald Trump Over Calling Meryl Streep 'Overrated'." *PEOPLE.com.* Time Inc, 10 Jan. 2017. Web.

Pilkington, Ed. "Ronald Reagan Had Alzheimer's While President, Says Son." *The Guardian.* Guardian News and Media, 17 Jan. 2011. Web.

"Politicians Are Still Trusted Less than Estate Agents, Journalists and Bankers." *Ipsos MORI.* N.p., n.d. Web.

"Pornhub's 2015 Year in Review." *Pornhub's 2015 Year in Review – Pornhub Insights.* Pornhub, 04 Apr. 2016. Web.

Pramuk, Jacob. "What Trump and Clinton Spent per Electoral Vote." *CNBC.* CNBC, 09 Dec. 2016. Web.

Pruitt, Sarah. "5 Things You May Not Know About Lincoln, Slavery and Emancipation." *History.com.* A&E Television Networks, 21 Sept. 2012. Web.

Rajghatta, Chidanand. "Reagan and India: Great Expectations - Times of India." *The Times of India*. N.p., 6 June 2004. Web.

Rascoe, Ayesha. "Trump to Sign Measure to Bolster U.S.'s Historically Black Colleges." *Reuters*. Thomson Reuters, 28 Feb. 2017. Web.

Rasmussen_Poll. "Daily Presidential Tracking Poll." *Rasmussen Reports*. N.p., n.d. Web.

Reagan, Courtney. "Ivanka Trump's Brand Saw HUGE Online Surge in February." *CNBC*. CNBC, 09 Mar. 2017. Web.

Revesz New York, Rachael. "Leonardo DiCaprio Flies 8,000 Miles in Private Jet to Accept 'green Award'." *The Independent*. Independent Digital News and Media, 22 May 2016. Web.

Revesz New York, Rachael. "Survey Finds Hillary Clinton Has 'more than 99% Chance' of Winning Election over Donald Trump." *The Independent*. Independent Digital News and Media, 05 Nov. 2016. Web.

Rogers, Thomas. "Inside the Creepy World of Neo-Nazi Hipsters." *Rolling Stone*. Rolling Stone, 23 June 2014. Web.

Root, Wayne Allyn. *Angry White Male: How the Donald Trump Phenomenon Is Changing America-- and What We Can All Do to Save the Middle Class*. Skyhorse Publishing, 2016.

Rosenthal, Phil. "ESPN Removes Robert Lee from Calling Virginia Game in Charlottesville Due to His Name." *Chicagotribune.com*. N.p., 23 Aug. 2017. Web.

Rossiter, Lyle H. *The Liberal Mind: The Psychological Causes of Political Madness*. N.p.: Free World , LLC, 2008. Print.

"Sectarianism in Pakistan." *Wikipedia*. Wikimedia Foundation, 18 Aug. 2017. Web.

Sharma, Dinesh. "Indian-Americans Back Obama in a Big Way." *Al Jazeera English*. N.p., n.d. Web.

Silver, Nate. "Why FiveThirtyEight Gave Trump A Better Chance Than Almost Anyone Else."

FiveThirtyEight. FiveThirtyEight, 11 Nov. 2016. Web.

Skelding, Conor. "Ben Carson: My Mom Kept Us out of Public Housing to Avoid 'danger'." *Politico PRO*. N.p., 08 Dec. 2016. Web.

Smith, Emily, and Daniel Halper. "Donald Trump's Media Summit Was a 'f——ing Firing Squad'." *New York Post*. New York Post, 22 Nov. 2016. Web.

Sparshott, Jeffrey. "U.S. Homeownership Rate Falls to Five-Decade Low." *The Wall Street Journal*. Dow Jones & Company, 29 July 2016. Web.

SpazzWagon. "The Rock - If You Smell What The Rock Is Cooking! 2011." *YouTube*. YouTube, 07 Mar. 2012. Web.

Sun-Times Media Wire. "9 Dead, 30 Wounded in Weekend Shootings across Chicago." *ABC7 Chicago*. N.p., 14 Aug. 2017. Web.

Taylor, Goldie. "Goldie Taylor-Bill Clinton's Ugly Defense Of His Crime Bill That Harmed Black

Communities." *The Daily Beast.* The Daily Beast Company, 09 Apr. 2016. Web.

TheExtremeEgnigmaV1. "The Rock 11th WWE Theme Song "Do You Smell It"." *YouTube.* YouTube, 29 June 2012. Web.

Timmerman, Kenneth R. "Huma Abedin's Ties to the Muslim Brotherhood." *TheHill.* N.p., 23 Aug. 2016. Web.

Tyson, Alec, and Shiva Maniam. "Behind Trump's Victory: Divisions by Race, Gender, Education." *Pew Research Center.* N.p., 09 Nov. 2016. Web.

University, Quinnipiac. "QU Poll Release Detail." *QU Poll.* N.p., n.d. Web.

"US Politics Betting." *US Presidential Election 2020 - US Politics Betting and Election Betting from Paddy Power.* N.p., n.d. Web.

"US Presidential Election 2020 Winner Betting Odds | Politics." *Oddschecker.com.* N.p., n.d. Web.

"Virtue+Signalling." *Urban Dictionary,* www.urbandictionary.com/define.php?term=virtue%2Bsignalling.

Vissa, Naresh. *FIFTY SHADES OF MARKETING: Whip Your Business Into Shape & Dominate Your Competition.* N.p.: Krish, 2015. Print.

Vissa, Naresh, Jason Hartman, and Rob Walch. *Podcastnomics: The Book of Podcasting ... to Make You Millions.* N.p.: Krish, 2014. Print.

Vissa, Naresh. *THE NEW PR: 21st Century Public Relations Strategies & Resources... To Reach Millions.* N.p.: Krish, 2016. Web.

Vissa, Naresh. "Viewpoint: A Syracuse Alum on the Bernie Fine Scandal and the Future of Jim Boeheim." *USA Today.* Gannett Satellite Information Network, 19 June 2014. Web.

The Washington Post. WP Company, n.d. Web.

"Wayne Allyn Root Show." *USA Radio Network,* usaradio.com/wayne-allyn-root/.

Wayne Root, rootforamerica.com/.

White, Gillian B. "Education Gaps Don't Fully Explain Why Black Unemployment Is So High." *The*

Atlantic. Atlantic Media Company, 21 Dec. 2015. Web.

"The White Man's Burden": Kipling's Hymn to U.S. Imperialism." *HISTORY MATTERS - The U.S. Survey Course on the Web.* N.p., n.d. Web.

"White Men Can't Jump (1992)." *IMDb.* IMDb.com, n.d. Web.

Wren, Adam, Brandon Ambrosino, Jack Shafer, and Kimberly Chrisman-Campbell. "Undecided? Really? Five Undecided Voters Explain." *POLITICO Magazine.* N.p., 05 Nov. 2016. Web.

Wright, Kai. "Black Life and Death in the Age of Obama." *The Nation.* N.p., 05 Jan. 2017. Web.

Yousterqiu. "Bill Clinton Checks out Melania Trump during Inauguration." *YouTube.* YouTube, 20 Jan. 2017. Web.

Zanotti, Emily. "Canceled Classes, a Cry-in and More: College Campuses Reel from Trump Win." *Fox News.* FOX News Network, 10 Nov. 2016. Web.